Using
Illustrations
to Preach
with
Power

Using Illustrations to Preach with Power

Bryan Chapell

ZondervanPublishingHouse
Academic and Professional Books
Grand Rapids, Michigan

A Division of HarperCollins*Publishers*

Using Illustrations to Preach with Power
Copyright © 1992 by Bryan Chapell

Requests for information should be addressed to:
Zondervan Publishing House
Academic and Professional Books
Grand Rapids, Michigan 49530

Library of Congress Cataloging-in-Publication Data

Chapell, Bryan.
    Using illustrations to preach with power / Bryan Chapell.
      p.   cm.
    Includes bibliographical references.
    ISBN 0-310-58461-2
    1. Preaching.   2. Homiletical illustrations.   I. Title.
BV4226.C43   1992
251'.08–dc20   92-29988
                                                                  CIP

Edited by Verlyn D. Verbrugge
Cover designed by Jody Langley

Printed in the United States of America

92 93 94 95 96 97 / CH / 10 9 8 7 6 5 4 3 2 1

To my wife, Kathy,
whose love secures our family with such strength
that I am able to embark on projects such as this.

Acknowledgments

* * *

Thanks for this work are extended:

To Covenant Theological Seminary,
which has given me the great privilege
of teaching others the wonder
of preaching the Word of God.

To Mrs. June Dare, whose tireless
secretarial efforts enable me to do
so much more than I
have a right to expect.

To my Sovereign Lord,
who made me his child
at the cost of his Son.

Contents

Wizened or Wise?

I was preaching on the Incarnation from the second chapter of Philippians. I wanted my congregation to understand the rich implications of Christ's humanity without falling into the ancient trap of diminishing his deity. I waxed long and carefully over the correct understanding of the seventh verse, where the ancient hymn records that Jesus "made himself nothing." I even got a bit excited about the original language wording. I pounded my fist on the pulpit to emphasize a proper understanding of the Greek term *kenosis*. But the congregation seemed to share little of my excitement. I went home questioning whether, despite my fervor, anyone knew anything more than when they entered church that Sunday. I had the sneaking suspicion that more than one spouse asked the other on the way home what the pastor was so worked up about that morning—only to be answered by shrugged shoulders.

A few weeks after my *kenosis* sermon, our church hosted a missions conference. Paul and Carolyn London from Sudan

Interior Mission were our speakers. To my horror, on the first Sunday morning of the conference Paul announced that he would be preaching on the same passage of Philippians I had so recently expounded. I feared the congregation would be frustrated at this redundancy since I had just explained the text so thoroughly. My fears initially seemed to be confirmed. The missionary began his message by emphasizing the continuing divinity of Christ just as I had. He narrowed his exposition to verse 7 just as I had. Then, however, his preaching took a different turn. Instead of concentrating on the Greek translation, the experienced missionary explained the text this way:

Where Carolyn and I minister in Africa the strongest man of the tribe is the chief. You might think this is because the chief must wear a very large headdress and heavy ceremonial robes, but there are other reasons, as you shall soon see.

Water is very scarce where these people live, so they have to dig deep wells. These are not wells as we know them—with brick walls, a pulley, and a bucket at the end of a rope. The African people sink a narrow well shaft as much as 100 feet into the ground. Even though the well is deep, the ground water of that dry land seeps very slowly into it and there is never a drop to waste. If the water were too easy to reach, the people might not use it sparingly, or an enemy might steal the next day's supply at night. So, the tribesmen cut alternating slits into the wall of the well all the way down to the water. By alternating his weight from one leg to the other, a man can use these slits as steps to walk down the shaft to the water. Only the largest, strongest men can make the arduous climb down the well and back up again with a full water skin for the whole tribe.

One day a man carrying water out of the shaft fell and broke his leg. He lay at the bottom of the well. No one dared to help because no one had the strength to make the climb carrying another man. The chief was summoned. When he saw the plight of the injured man, he doffed his massive headdress and discarded his ceremonial robe. Then the chief climbed down into the well, took the weight of the injured man on himself, and brought the man to safety. The chief did what no one else could do.

This is just what Jesus did for us. He came down to rescue us by taking the weight of our sin on himself. He put aside his heavenly honors, just as the chief put aside his headdress and robe, in order to save us. But let me ask you a question, friends. When that chief took off his headdress and robe, did he stop being the chief? No, of course not. In the same way, when Jesus "made himself nothing" and put aside his heavenly glory, he never ceased being God.

I stood beside Paul London as he shook hands with the people leaving church that morning. Almost everyone said something about the story he told. The most common comment was, "I never understood that verse until you explained it that way." No one was trying to insult me. Probably not one in fifty even remembered my *kenosis* epic. But now they not only remembered the Scripture, they understood it. The missionary's illustration had more than entertained. It had communicated biblical truth effectively—more effectively than my propositions.

The experience shook me because it challenged some of my basic assumptions about preaching. Only a few weeks earlier I had nodded in agreement when a wizened visiting professor leaned back in his armchair in our den and began a ten-minute complaint against the faults of current preaching—chief among them the use of illustrations. "All we do is entertain people," he said. "It is not enough just to preach. Now we must tell stories and be comedians. It's all because of TV. People just cannot sit and think anymore. We have to parade illustrations before them like hosts of a variety show. I will sprinkle some illustrations in my sermons because I must in order to make people listen, but how I hate it."

I had heard this attitude expressed many times. I accepted its validity in part because it was often expressed by those I respected. I also adopted the attitude because I could identify with this eminent scholar's discomfort over pandering to an audience's weaknesses in order to hold attention on God's Word. I have sensed the inappropriateness of my own calculated use of illustrations and have looked down on those who seem to rely on them without shame. Still, something wonderful had happened when Paul London spoke. The truth I valued had rung clearly in the hearts of my people, and I could sense no compromise in the man or the message.

My mind began to whirl with questions I previously had not dared to ask. I expected the scholar to be right, yet I witnessed my congregation sharing little of his antipathy for illustrations. The church seemed to reflect attitudes common among evangelicals. Unless the preaching degenerates into "just telling stories," people do not complain about the illustrative content of sermons. In fact, congregations seem to think illustrations are the most memorable, informative, and moving portions of many sermons. Is this because laypeople just do not appreciate good preaching? Is it, as the professor suggested, because television dominates the expectations and diminishes the capabilities of the modern mind? Or, could it be that illustrations contain a hidden dynamic of living truth that captures attention and furthers understanding in a way that no other sermonic tool can match? Such was my dilemma: Should I believe my colleague or my experience with the Londons?

The more I considered the contrast in my own recent experience and the scholar's assessment, the more questions I had. The use of illustrations has persisted through nearly two thousand years of Western preaching. My mailbox still overflows weekly with advertisements for periodicals, card catalogs, and computer services that market sermonic illustrations. Preachers as well as laypeople seem to have an almost insatiable appetite for this material. Have so many abandoned solid preaching, or do they instinctively know illustrations make their preaching more effective? As a conscientious preacher I recognized that, while responsible, biblical preaching must never pander to worldly pragmatics, neither must it reject an age-old tool without fully evaluating its usefulness. My search for some answers about the value of illustrations led to some unanticipated conclusions, which are the foundation of this book.

I discovered that today's congregations are not necessarily more dependent on illustrations than their Christian predecessors. Television has certainly changed our public-speaking expectations, but it does not seem radically to have changed the way the human mind functions and processes information. The mind yearns for, and needs, the concrete to anchor the abstract.

To say that illustrations aid the intellect, however, does not mean that they are merely a cognitive crutch. Illustrations are not supplemental to good exposition; they are a necessary form of exposition in which biblical truths are explained to the emotions and the will as well as to the intellect. Illustrations will not allow mere head knowledge. They exegete Scripture in the terms of human experience to create a whole-person understanding of God's Word. By framing biblical truths in the world in which we live and move and have our being, illustrations unite our personalities, our pasts, our present, our affections, our fears, our frustrations, our hopes, our hearts, our minds, and our souls in the understanding of that which is divine. They are integral to effective preaching, not because they entertain, but because they expand and deepen the applications the mind and heart can make.

The purpose of this book is to demonstrate why and how illustrations can be used in biblical preaching. My motivation is twofold: (1) I want to share an appreciation for the ways in which the effective use of illustrations can reach the people of God with the truths of his Word; and (2) I love the truths of God's Word more than illustrations. The complaint of my senior colleague is not without basis. Illustrations can be, and often are, used for all the wrong reasons. If this book can help provide insight into the proper use and development of illustrations in biblical preaching, then perhaps we can avoid the uses that damage our messages and preach with greater clarity of content and purity of purpose.

The time that Paul London spoke need not be a magic moment. The power and integrity with which he expressed the Word of God can be duplicated. This does not diminish the wonderful impact of his words. It gives us hope that our words can be just as effective when we understand the illustrative tools he so masterfully employed.

Part One

Background and Theory: Deciding About Illustrations

Chapter 1

The Art and the Argument

CRISIS IN PREACHING

Widespread dissatisfaction with preaching cuts across our churches. The disenchantment began to boil to the surface almost a generation ago. Young and old alike complained of preaching that was lost in abstraction, buried in jargon, and frozen in formula words incapable of firing the courage or of forging the answers needed for an age of unprecedented change. Thoughts too lofty to touch the realities of life precipitated criticism, the like of which American preachers had not endured since battles over slavery eroded public reverence for pulpit robes. Preachers cried for answers. Experts studied, surveyed, and assessed.

Clyde Reid offered the persepctive of religious professionals:

(1) Preachers tend to use complex, archaic language which the average person does not understand; (2) most sermons today are dull, boring, and uninteresting; (3) most preaching today is

irrelevant; (4) preaching today is not courageous preaching; (5) preaching does not communicate; (6) preaching does not lead to change in persons; (7) preaching has been overemphasized.

Reuel Howe spoke to laypeople and catalogued similar complaints:

(1) sermons often contain too many complex ideas; (2) sermons have too much analysis and too little answer; (3) sermons are too formal and too impersonal; (4) sermons use too much theological jargon; (5) sermons are too propositional, not enough illustrations; (6) too many sermons simply reach a dead end and give no guidance to commitment and action.[1]

The crisis continues. These seminal surveys and many subsequent studies have triggered an explosion of works advocating novel approaches to preaching. Baby and bathwater often seem flung out the back door together in this rush to develop new forms. Time will tell whether the new approaches have enduring value. What is obvious now is that no one is satisfied. The willingness of so many to experiment with so important a spiritual task highlights how desperate many consider their situation. Both pulpit and pew echo the concern that too many sermons have no direct connection with everyday life.

This book contends that preachers who properly develop and use life-situation illustrations in expository messages already possess a powerful corrective for the crisis in contemporary preaching. Such illustrations live where people live. They communicate meaning by common experience and, thus, do not allow biblical truths to fly over heads or reside in the surreal world of doctrinal jargon and abstract principle. Through this vehicle, true communication takes place and sermons themselves are filled with vibrant life.

DEFINITIONS

Preachers searching for illustrative materials soon find a variety of options available to use in their messages. The array of alternatives can itself create important questions about the types of illustrative content that best suit a sermon. The following heirarchy ranks such material by its complexity and relative emphasis on lived-body (i.e., descriptive) details:[2]

An Illustrative Hierarchy
Novelle
Allegory
Parable
Illustration
Allusion
Example
Analogy
Figures of Speech

The illustrative materials listed lower than "Illustration" on this hierarchy are characterized by their brevity. Figures, analogies, and examples can add rich expression to a sermon, but they do not involve listeners to the same degree as do true illustrations. A quote from an ancient saint or a statistic from a contemporary newspaper may add interest to a sermon, but neither carries the listener into a tangible understanding of a message as effectively as a full illustration. On the other hand, the categories of illustrative material higher than "Illustration" usually have greater length than is appropriate for sermons or reflect a particular literary genre conforming to conventions not typical of most sermons.[3] The aspect of the heirarchy most ideally suited to relevant preaching—preaching that communicates the powerful and living Word of God most effectively to its audience—is illustration.

A brief definition of true illustrations is as follows: Illustrations are "life-situation" stories within sermons whose details (whether explicitly told or imaginatively elicited) allow listeners to identify with an experience that elaborates, develops, and explains scriptural principles.[4] Through the details of the story, the listener is able imaginatively to enter an experience in which a sermonic truth can be observed. The preacher tells the what, when, where, and why of an occurrence to give listeners personal access to the occasion. He encourages each listener to see, feel, taste, or smell features of an event as though he or she were bodily present in the unfolding account. Then, along with these sensory details, the preacher also suggests the emotions, thoughts, or reactions that would typify the experience of one living the account.

These life and body descriptions create the "lived-body" details that distinguish true illustration from mere allusion or example. In both allusion and example the speaker refers to an account, whereas in an illustration the preacher invites the listener into the experience. The lived-body details flesh out the illustration in such a way that the listener can vicariously enter the narrative world of the illustration.[5] It is true that listeners can supply details out of their own imaginations to experience a concept to which the preacher refers in an example or an allusion. The categories cannot be strictly drawn. The point is that in examples and allusions the listener primarily supplies the lived-body details, whereas in true illustrations the preacher supplies them.

Illustrations, therefore, lead listeners into events. In an example the preacher says, "I have observed. . . ." In an allusion the preacher says, "This reminds me of. . . ." With an illustration the preacher says, "I'll take you there." In essence, when the preacher illustrates, he says, "You will know what I mean by comparing this to a memory from your life," or "Live through this new experience with me so you will know." This means that illustrations, however briefly expressed, reflect life-stories. Whether the account is new to the listener or conjured from memory, the preacher verbally re-creates a slice of life that defines a sermon's ideas.

HISTORICAL OVERVIEW

It would be incorrect to suggest that ours is the first generation to discover the value of using illustrations in preaching. We need but glimpse at the best preaching of practically every era in the history of the church to discern illustrations' value. With rare exceptions the most esteemed preaching has consistently relied on the vision of the inner eye.

Had not the apostle Paul punctuated his words with images of the full armor of God, the race course, and the altar to an unknown God, we would strain to remember his instruction. Had not Jonathan Edwards dangled sinful spiders over the pit of flame, no one would know "Sinners in the Hands of an Angry God." If William Jennings Bryan had not decried, "You shall not crucify mankind upon a cross of gold," his political "sermon" would have been forgotten the next day. If Martin Luther King, Jr., had not led us through a "dream" and onto a "mountaintop," the march on Washington might have become nothing more than a ragged hike across a majestic mall.

Books have extolled the sensory appeals of Charles Spurgeon, the images of Peter Marshall, the characterizations of Clovis Chappell, and the human dramas of Harry Emerson Fosdick. None of these men, of widely varying theological perspectives, preached in times dominated by visual electronics, yet they dressed their sermons in strong illustrative images with powerful results. Prior to our contemporary "age of visual literacy,"[6] these preaching giants tapped something deep and fundamental in human understanding. We are just beginning to discover in scientific terms what this fundamental something is.

Hidden Prejudice

Many recent studies support the use of sermonic storytelling and illustration by citing the long tradition of their use. Contemporary insights into the narrative structure of Scripture have spawned a spate of books and articles defending the use of stories in sermons and organic "story sermons."[7] Other works explore the role of storytelling and illustration in various preaching traditions in order to prove their use is neither novel nor damaging.[8] Unfortunately, such an appeal to past works potentially reinforces a hidden prejudice that these devices are the preaching forms of preliterate, unlearned, or folk cultures and are thus ill-suited to today's sophisticated audiences.

The twentieth century's classic textbooks on preaching often stereotype illustration as primitive or elementary. Henry Grady Davis reflects this attitude in his *Design for Preaching*, the most widely used homiletics textbook of the last hundred years:[9]

> Again it is contended that illustrative stories are necessary to supply interest, to give the human touch, and to make the message relevant to concrete human situations. The answer is the same. What does this imply concerning the texture of the thought before and after the story? . . . If the preacher has something relevant to say, and if the fabric of his thought is a woof of particulars on a warp of clear generalizations, his sermon will need no artificial adornments to make it interesting.
>
> Further it is said illustrative stories are needed to supply pauses and resting places for listeners in the progress of the sermon's movement. This is by all odds the most valid claim made for them, in my opinion. That they are necessary in the contemporary sermon, however, is a dubious argument.[10]

For this premier homiletician, illustrations are popular frill rather than an essential element of excellent preaching. His cautions and qualifications virtually outlaw illustrations from "quality" preaching.

Other classic texts of the century show less antipathy to illustrations than Davis, but they reflect his prejudice nonetheless. John Broadus devotes just thirteen pages to illustration in his massive *On the Preparation and Delivery of Sermons*—and the last two pages of the chapter are cautions. More revealing, he begins his discussion with this "faint praise":

> Strictly speaking, one would not call illustration a distinct element of the sermon co-ordinate with explanation and argument, or with persuasion, which will be studied in the next chapter. Its function is *solely auxiliary*, coming to the support now

of one and now of another of the principal elements [emphasis added].[11]

Such a lukewarm introduction hardly fires serious consideration of the subject.

Illustration receives a little more favorable treatment in Ilion T. Jones's still popular *Principles and Practice of Preaching*. His chapter—also relatively short—on illustration begins, "Illustrations are essential because of the way the human mind functions."[12] This auspicious beginning makes the following lines all the more disappointing:

> Abstract statements of truth, detached from the practical experiences of real people in live human situations, have little power to convince ordinary minds. . . . It is safe to say that the great masses of the people do not think—are not prepared to think— in exact, carefully worded formulas.[13]

Jones has excellent insights into the practice of illustrating, but he only considers illustrations "essential" because preachers must accommodate people with "ordinary" minds who are "not prepared to think." In this light, illustration remains a demeaning chore.

Most newer textbooks still relegate illustrations to the category of "preaching aids,"[14] though some offer exceptionally valuable insight into their use.[15] An attitude of reservation pervades the advice on illustration given to prudent preachers.

Holy Pollutants

There are good reasons for caution. Though the marketing of illustrations is as old as the collections of "exempla" that flourished in Medieval Europe,[16] no one has yet found a way to control the mania that often accompanies them.[17] Where there are illustrations there are showmen, and where there are showmen there are charlatans. Ralph Lewis, for example, records the performance of a contemporary preacher who jumped on the pulpit and rode it as a camel going "Whumpf! Whumpf! Whumpf!" over eight-hundred miles of imaginary desert dunes, imitating Eleazer's quest to find a bride for Isaac.[18]

Such antics are not new—nor extreme by some ancient standards. Catharine Regan records the medieval cases of a friar who surrounded his pulpit with decomposing bodies for illustrative impact and of a preacher who, with a magician's timing, would withdraw a skull from under his cloak.[19] It may seem unnecessary to assert that the potential for abuse should not preclude their use, for the obvious excesses of the past need not be mimicked in order for illustrations to be of value today. But in the ministry, where the integrity of speakers and the purity of messages are of utmost importance, past errors greatly influence present thought.

For the best of motives preachers may conscientiously shun any appearance of popularizing a message lest truth appear to be compromised for appeal. After all, the apostle Paul urged that preaching not be characterized by "enticing words" (1 Cor. 2:4), "flattering words" (1 Thess. 2:5), or "the wisdom of this world" (1 Cor. 2:6). No doubt these apostolic injunctions have inhibited the use of communication tools that are perceived as mere "rhetorical devices." Godly pastors are rightly concerned that worldly wisdom or popular artifice not pollute biblical preaching. Unfortunately, such concerns are often translated to mean that a message that appeals to an audience, or is readily understood, is somehow inherently flawed. These are matters of attitude and opinion that may sound ridiculous to nonpastors, but they cannot help but affect the conscientious preacher who would rather fail than manipulate.

In addition to the possibility of manipulating audiences, the use of illustrations has sometimes raised suspicions because of its propensity for manhandling truth. For example, medieval interpreters asserted that a variety of allegorical meanings underlay every biblical text. A literal interpretation based upon grammatical-historical insights was considered simplistic. The approaches considered more profitable attempted to expose hidden, spiritual meanings behind the plain sense of every biblical statement or object. The intent of the author was not as important as allegorical insight in determining what a text meant. Analogy piled upon analogy led to wild interpretations that left the church with few biblical anchors since a text could mean whatever a good imagination determined. The Protestant Reformers of the sixteenth and seventeenth centuries rebelled against this hermeneutic, as Augustine had centuries before (in theory more than in actual practice) in early Catholicism and as modern Catholics have done again in the nineteenth and twentieth centuries.

Centuries of effort to rid the church of allegorical impreci-sion has resulted in a latent suspicion of all analogies—including illustrations. Preachers must understand this back-ground to use illustrations intelligently. To use the words of Ralph Lewis:

> Analogy ran amuck for centuries, plaguing the Christian church with wild excesses. Legitimate Bible analogy slid to absurd depths when preachers allowed their imaginations to race without restraint, reason or responsibility. . . .
>
> Such excesses led to the basic exegetical principle of the Reformation insisting every Scripture passage has but one meaning. John Calvin championed the cause against allegories. Luther too said, "Origen's allegories are not worth so much dirt."
>
> The conflict in the church persists. . . . It's true that freedom to expand meaning has often become license to distort truth with illusory fancy, fiction and figments. Yet scriptural models suggest there must be a legitimate use of analogy. While the ministerial record warrants caution with this technique, analogy can be another effective inductive ingredient in sermons.[20]

DISCOVERIES OF THE TRAILBLAZERS

We can be thankful that three recent approaches to preaching have moved in the direction of supporting the use of illustrations by highlighting the importance of linking under-standing to experience. Each trailblazing effort more clearly marks a fundamental role for illustrations.

Inductive Preaching

The first school is "inductive preaching." An inductive sermon focuses on particular human dilemmas, personal problems, or common concerns that help listeners discover scriptural truths. In contrast to a deductive sermon that tries to prove doctrinal principles before making specific applications, inductive messages start with the human need. The sermon and its major divisions typically try to lead to conclusions on a personal level rather than prove universal principles. Particulars take precedence over propositions. Interest and relevance drive the message as doctrinal answers unfold. Whereas logical proof and expositional argument dominate a traditional deductive sermon, personal concerns and real-life experiences highlight inductive approaches.

Two well-known works on inductive preaching are Fred B. Craddock's *as one without authority*[21] [*sic*] and Ralph Lewis's *Inductive Preaching* (co-authored with son Gregg Lewis). Though they come with differing theological perspectives, both authors conclude that Scripture consistently gives greater attention to personalities and particulars than to propositions and principles. Both authors question whether traditional Western preaching consistently reflects this scriptural model and mind. Lewis asks:

> Could our longstanding practice of deductive method be part of our problem in winning involvement in our preaching today? Could deduction be a contribution to the feeling many laypersons have that sermons tend to drone along one flight above reality? Could a re-thinking of sermon structure provide any help or hope?
>
> . . . Inductive preaching can do those things. So why have we ignored the potential of inductive structure and logic in our sermons?
>
> Induction begins with the particulars of life experience and points toward principles, concepts, conclusions. The inductive course can grow out of the hearers' needs rather than the uncertainty of the preacher. The preacher seeks to lead rather

than push. He explores with the people before he explains what they find. Inductive preaching is a quest for discovery. It can disarm, interest and involve the people in the exploration and capitalize on the psychological process of learning from experience.[22]

In other words, inductive preaching links a sermon's effectiveness to the real-life associations it contains.

But two problems confront inductive preaching. The first is the matter of authority. Because the inductive process emphasizes matters not directly off the pages of Scripture, it raises suspicions similar to those faced above. Even worse, while illustrations attempt to illuminate exposition, the inductive approach deemphasizes (or, at least delays) authoritative conclusions based on divine revelation. This does not sit well in evangelical circles.[23]

The second problem is inertia—that is, resistance to change. While Lewis contends that the best preaching throughout history is inductive, he is hard-pressed to find examples; he offers mainly those of preachers using illustrations in traditional sermon formats.[24] Both Craddock and Lewis ultimately admit that Western preaching in general is unlikely to embrace the inductive style any time soon. The best they can hope for is that their approach will supplement traditional approaches.[25] The older forms of preaching are not easily overcome and, given their two thousand years of usefulness, probably this is appropriate. The proponents of inductive preaching may have made a better case for elevating elements of traditional sermons that involve listeners than for creating a different type of sermon.

Narrative Preaching

Another novel approach to preaching takes advantage of the burgeoning research in narrative theory. Craddock writes:

Actually in good preaching what is referred to as illustrations are, in fact, stories or anecdotes which do not illustrate the point;

rather they are the point. In other words, a story may carry in its bosom the whole message rather than the illumination of a message which had already been related in another but less clear way.[26]

If, as many now suggest, illustrations are stories in either elaborated or embryonic form, then narrative theory can help us determine how they communicate so efficiently and deeply.

Narrative theory presumes that a community's most basic values are stored, transmitted, and communicated through stories. Researchers have discovered that the most simple expressions have nearly infinite interpretive possibilities based upon the varying definitions, nuances, contexts, and motives that can characterize every word. For the words to make sense to more than one person, they must arise from the contexts of shared experiences. Narratives provide such contexts. A community's stories are the dictionaries that define words through experiences everyone recognizes. Thus, shared stories enable persons to think and act in common.[27]

Narrative theory often explores the ways in which religious stories can help us better interpret, understand, and share spiritual truths. Unfortunately, few of these studies offer concrete guidance on how the principles of narrative, uncovered in the biblical record, can help the communication of spiritual truths today.[28] One senses that the narrative theorists have a unique perspective on preaching that may shake traditional notions and patterns, but so far they offer little concrete guidance on how this Sunday's sermon should change.[29] However, if the theorists are correct, illustrations in story form possess extraordinary communication power. We need only determine how to tap it.

Life-Situation Preaching

Stories make sermons understandable *and* relevant. This brings us to the third school of thought that underscores the value of illustrations—life-situation preaching. This approach was pioneered by Harold W. Ruopp in the thirties and forties, popularized by Charles F. Kemp in the fifties and sixties, and revitalized in the eighties by Lloyd M. Perry and Charles Sell. Life-situation preaching "strives to reach into the core of distress in personal, modern living and apply the healing of the gospel."[30]

Practitioners of life-situation sermons recognize that when "preaching is directed to people in definite situations with specific needs," messages are more relevant, powerful, and potentially helpful. Robert J. McCracken's definition of life-situation preaching spells out the emphasis:

> Seeking to avoid the remoteness and irrelevance, not to say unreality of much biblical exposition, it starts with people where they are, which was what Jesus did over and over again. The point of departure is a live issue of some kind. It may be personal or social; it may be theological or ethical. Whatever it is, the preacher makes it his business to get at the core of the problem, and, that done, he goes on to work out the solution, with biblical revelation, and the mind and Spirit of Christ, as the constraint points of reference and direction.[31]

This definition of life-situation preaching offers distinctives that are also helpful in defining one type of illustration. Though there is no standard definition of what a "life-situation illustration" might be, the philosophy behind "life-situation preaching" suggests some possibilities. Life-situation illustrations would be those that reflect the real problems and common emotions confronted by ordinary persons as they seek to apply biblical principles to common or extraordinary experiences.

In other contexts, such illustrations might be known as "human interest accounts," but when they are identified as *life-situation* illustrations, preachers are more likely to see their value.[32] A life-situation illustration showing persons applying biblical truths to real-world circumstances captures those truths in the most relevant, realistic, and approachable terms. Criticisms of irrelevancy ring hollow. Truth is removed from the ethereal world of abstract dogma. Scripture becomes real, accessible, and meaningful because its message gets rooted in real life.

The chief concern with this approach to preaching is that, as traditionally advocated, it is weak on exposition of the Bible. The sermon revolves around the life situation, and whatever is said about the Scriptures is often tangential to the message rather than its central core. The approach advocated in the present book intends to integrate life situations with the exegesis of the Word of God and with biblical propositions.

A Unifying Theory

These three modern preaching schools are subsumed under a more ancient tradition—illustration—and imply the power of that tool. The diverse threads of thought weave a consistent pattern: understanding requires experience, a maxim that we will explore more thoroughly in chapter 3. This fundamental assumption underlying these schools suggests that illustrations may hold the key to addressing their concerns while simultaneously addressing the ineffectiveness of much contemporary preaching. In other words, life-situation illustrations can revitalize the traditional forms without challenging them and, thus, avoid the hostility and inertia more revolutionary methods have confronted.

A CONCLUDING ILLUSTRATION

A missionary to Uganda recently told how he came to understand that what is often decried for its abuse may not necessarily need to be denied use. His wife was invited to a rural village to play piano for a worship service. While she was traveling to the remote church, an unseasonable rainstorm deluged the village and the shelter the people had erected for the service. The piano was so thoroughly doused that it was unplayable. The villagers adjusted by accompanying the hymns of the worship service with some of their traditional tortoise-shell instruments. One of the church's elders later profusely apologized to the missionary's wife for his people's use of tribal instruments in accompanying the Christian hymns. She was confused by his embarrassment and asked why he would apologize for using instruments that added such a wonderful, cultural flavor to a worship tradition that is usually so foreign to his people. "Don't you know?" asked the elder. "My people have sometimes used tortoise-shell instruments in devil worship!" "Oh," replied the smiling missionary, "you should see how my people have sometimes used pianos."

Remembering that simply because an instrument can be used for the wrong purposes does not make the instrument itself wrong will help allay many worries about the use of illustrations in biblical preaching.

Standing in tension are two legitimate concerns. The first is that the biblical content of a sermon may be diluted by undue emphasis on the extrabiblical material upon which illustration-oriented preachers depend. The second equally legitimate concern is that sermons whose chief priorities are exegetical may be too dry for congregational consumption without the communication benefits that illustrations provide. The first concern is that biblical truth *will not be heard* with illustrations. The latter concern is that biblical truth *cannot be heard* without illustrations. Several scholars have chronicled the debate,[33] but it will not cease unless someone provides convincing proof that using illustrations does not automatically distort or diminish biblical truth. To that task this book has been dedicated.

Notes

1. These quotations are taken from Byron Val Johnson, "A Media Selection Model for Use with a Homiletical Taxonomy" (Ph.D. diss.; Cardondale: Southern Illinois University, 1982), p. 215.
2. James D. Robertson, "Sermon Illustration and the Use of Resources," section 2 of *Baker's Dictionary of Practical Theology*, ed. Ralph G. Turnbull (Grand Rapids: Baker, 1967); rpt. in Vernon L. Stanfield et al., *Homiletics* (Grand Rapids: Baker, 1972), pp. 46–49.
3. J. Daniel Baumann offers a similar hierarchy, calling illustrations in simplest form "ejaculatory examples," in slightly more complex

forms "figures of speech" and "analogy," and in the most artistic forms "parable," "historical allusion," and "anecdotes" (*An Introduction to Contemporary Preaching* [Grand Rapids: Baker, 1972], pp. 173–74).

4. Because he so fears the term *illustration* will be confused with lesser forms of illustrative material, Jay Adams eschews the use of the word entirely and opts instead for the word *story* as the term that most accurately communicates the essentials of illustration (*Preaching with Purpose: A Comprehensive Textbook on Biblical Preaching* [Grand Rapids: Baker, 1982], pp. 90–91).

5. Fred B. Craddock, *Preaching* (Nashville: Abingdon, 1985), p. 204.

6. Ralph L. Lewis with Gregg Lewis, *Inductive Preaching: Helping People Listen* (Westchester, Ill.: Crossway, 1983), p. 10.

7. See George M. Bass, "The Story Sermon: Key to Effective Preaching," *Preaching* 2, 4 (1987), p. 36; William J. Bausch, *Storytelling Imagination and Faith* (Mystic, Conn.: Twenty-third, 1984); Richard L. Eslinger, *A New Hearing: Living Options in Homiletic Method* (Nashville: Abingdon, 1987); Leslie B. Flynn, *Come Alive with Illustrations: How to Find, Use, and File Good Stories for Sermons and Speeches* (Grand Rapids: Baker, 1987); Michael J. Hostetler, *Illustrating the Sermon*, in The Craft of Preaching Series (Grand Rapids: Zondervan, 1989); Wayne Bradley Robinson, ed., *Journeys Toward Narrative Preaching* (New York: Pilgrim, 1990); Bruce C. Salmon, *Storytelling in Preaching: A Guide to the Theory and Practice* (Nashville: Broadman, 1988).

8. Dwight Conquergood, "Literacy and Oral Performance in Anglo-Saxon England: Conflict and Confluence of Traditions," in *Performance of Literature in Historical Perspectives*, ed. David W. Thompson (Lanham, Md.: University Press of America, 1983), pp. 10–145; Henry H. Mitchell, *The Recovery of Preaching* (New York: Harper and Row, 1977); Bruce A. Rosenberg, *The Art of the American Folk Preacher* (New York: Oxford University Press, 1970); cf. Phyllis Alsdurf, "Preaching at the Guthrie Theater," *Christianity Today* 31 (July 10, 1987), pp. 58–60.

9. A. Duane Litfin, "The Five Most-Used Homiletics Texts," *Christianity Today* 17 (1973), p. 1138. Litfin's assessment of works used through the century should not imply that more recent books such as those by Haddon Robinson and Fred Craddock will fail to challenge sales of the classic texts as this century concludes.

10. Henry Grady Davis, *Design for Preaching* (Philadelphia: Fortress, 1958), p. 257.

11. John A. Broadus, *On the Preparation and Delivery of Sermons* (New York: Harper and Row, 1944), p. 196.

12. Ilion T. Jones, *Principles and Practice of Preaching* (New York: Abingdon, 1956), p. 136.
13. Ibid.
14. A survey should include: Jay E. Adams, *Preaching with Purpose*; Fred Craddock, *Preaching*; James Cox, *Preaching: A Comprehensive Approach to the Design and Delivery of Sermons* (New York: Harper and Row, 1985); Henry J. Eggold, *Preaching Is Dialogue: A Concise Introduction to Homiletics* (Grand Rapids: Baker, 1980); John Killinger, *Fundamentals of Preaching* (Philadelphia: Fortress, 1985); Woodrow Michael Kroll, *Prescription for Preaching* (Grand Rapids: Baker, 1980); Ralph L. Lewis with Gregg Lewis, *Inductive Preaching*; Edward F. Marquart, *Quest for Better Preaching* (Minneapolis: Augsburg, 1985); Lloyd M. Perry and Charles M. Sell, *Speaking to Life's Problems: A Sourcebook for Preaching and Teaching* (Chicago: Moody Press, 1983); Ian Pitt-Watson, *A Primer for Preachers* (Grand Rapids: Baker, 1986); Haddon W. Robinson, *Biblical Preaching: The Development and Delivery of Expository Messages* (Grand Rapids: Baker, 1980); Hans Van Der Geest, *Presence in the Pulpit: The Impact of Personality in Preaching*, trans. Douglas W. Stott (Atlanta: John Knox, 1981); Jerry Vines, *A Practical Guide to Sermon Preparation* (Chicago: Moody Press, 1985).
15. See especially Adams, *Preaching with Power*; Kroll, *Prescription for Preaching*; Lewis, *Inductive Preaching*; and Robinson, *Biblical Preaching*.
16. James J. Murphy, *Medieval Rhetoric: A Select Bibliography* (Toronto: University of Toronto Press, 1971), pp. 80–81; see also Murphy's more exhaustive work, *Rhetoric in the Middle Ages: A History of Rhetorical Theory from Saint Augustine to the Renaissance* (Berkeley: University of California Press, 1974); and Belden C. Lane, "Rabbinical Stories: A Primer on Theological Method," *The Christian Century* 98 (1981), pp. 1306–9.
17. Murphy, *Medieval Rhetoric*, pp. 71, 80–81.
18. Lewis, *Inductive Preaching*, p. 36.
19. Catharine A. Regan, "Liturgy and Preaching as Oral Context for Medieval English Literature," *Performance of Literature in Historical Perspectives*, ed. David W. Thompson (Lanham, Md.: University Press of America, 1983), p. 171.
20. Lewis, *Inductive Preaching*, p. 39. Lewis defines analogy as "an inductive technique that explains the unknown by the better known," exemplified in the biblical use of such illustrative "images as a tree, bride, building, cornerstone, sheep, shepherd and water."
21. Fred B. Craddock, *as one without authority* (Enid, Okla.: Phillips University Press, 1974).

22. Lewis, *Inductive Preaching*, p. 32.
23. Ibid., pp. 45, 56–57, 103.
24. Ibid., pp. 197ff.
25. Ibid., p. 32.
26. Craddock, *Preaching*, p. 204.
27. For a concise summary of narrative theory in theological discussion see Alister E. McGrath, "The Biography of God," *Christianity Today* 35 (July 22, 1991), pp. 22–24. A critical summary of narrative as a communication model is the focus of Walter Fisher's two-part series of articles on "The Narrative Paradigm" appearing in *Communication Monographs* in 1984 and 1985. Fisher argues from both secular and religious sources "that symbols are created and communicated ultimately as stories meant to give order to human experience and to induce others to dwell in them to establish ways of living in common, in communities in which there is sanction for the story that constitutes one's life" (see his "Narration as a Human Communication Paradigm: The Case for Public Moral Argument," in *Communication Monographs* 51 [1984], p. 6). The philosophical foundations of Fisher's work are discussed in the appendix of this book.
28. Ethel Barrett attempts such an approach to religious teaching in *Storytelling: It's Easy* (Grand Rapids: Zondervan, 1960), but the book is largely a reiteration of the rationale for the use of illustrations for traditional reasons rather than an application of contemporary narrative theory. Eugene Lowry, in *How to Preach a Parable: Designs for Narrative Sermons* (Nashville: Abingdon, 1989), *The Homiletical Plot: The Sermon as Narrative Art Form* (Atlanta: John Knox, 1980), and *Doing Time in the Pulpit: The Theology and Practice of Narrative Preaching* (Nashville: Abingdon, 1985), also gives guidelines for preaching on narrative passages and argues for a new understanding of why preaching should contain a better reflection of biblical structures. Much the same can be said of H. Stephen Shoemaker's *Retelling the Biblical Story: The Theology and Practice of Narrative Preaching* (Nashville: Broadman, 1985). Richard A. Jensen presents compelling arguments that demonstrate the weaknesses of strictly didactic preaching and offers some excellent models of sermons using narrative forms in *Telling the Story* (Minneapolis: Augsburg, 1980). Probably the best work to date which both considers reasons behind the dynamics of biblical narrative and specifically tries to apply those dynamics to regular preaching on many types of biblical literature is *Preaching the Story* by Edmund A. Steimle, Morris J.Niedenthal, and Charles L. Rice (Philadelphia: Fortress, 1980). Good summations of these approaches can be found in *Journeys Toward Narrative Preaching*, ed.

Wayne Bradley Robinson (New York: Pilgrim, 1990), and *A New Hearing: Living Options in Homiletic Method*, by Richard Eslinger (Nashville: Abingdon, 1987). A unique perspective that reflects many of the principles of narrative theory is found in Mark Ellingsen's *The Integrity of Biblical Narrative: Story in Theology and Proclamation* (Minneapolis: Fortress, 1990); he insists on using biblical stories alone as the primary vehicle for Gospel communication.

29. Cf. McGrath, "The Biography of God," p. 24. For notable exceptions that provide helpful possibilities, see Lowry, *The Homiletical Plot* and *How to Preach a Parable*, and James M. Wardlaw, ed., *Preaching Biblically: Creating Sermons in the Shape of Scripture* (Philadelphia: Westminster, 1983).

30. Perry and Sell, *Speaking to Life's Problems*, p. 9.

31. Ibid., p. 17.

32. Baumann uses the "life-situation" designation for illustrations that create immediate applications for contemporary life (see *An Introduction to Contemporary Preaching*, p. 250).

33. George M. Bass, "The Story Sermon: Key to Effective Preaching," pp. 33–34; Deane Kemper, *Effective Preaching* (Philadelphia: Westminster, 1985), p. 79; and Charles Duthie, in *My Way of Preaching*, ed. Robert J. Smithson (London: Pickering and Inglis, n.d.), p. 15, as quoted in John Killinger, *Fundamentals of Preaching*, p. 107.

Chapter 2

The Path of Scripture

REACHING THE WHOLE PERSON

More than anyone else, preachers should know that experience teaches, moves, and motivates beyond bare statements of doctrine. As we shall see in this chapter, the Spirit's communication of truth is not one dimensional, and neither should be the preaching that he empowers. It is true that the Gospel is logical, but it is also spiritual, visceral, and impressionistic. It calls believers to worship with all their heart and soul, as well as with their mind (Deut. 6:5; Matt. 22:37).

Reaching the Heart

The best preaching never relies on intellectual appeals alone because the Bible teaches that we are more than beings of pure mind. Preachers must reach for the heart, for out of the heart proceed the issues of life (Prov. 4:23). Emotions operating in isolation from thought are dangerous, but rationality barren of love, discretion, sensitivity, and even holy rage can also be contrary to godliness. God has placed emotions in us to help us interpret our lives, our world, and his Word. If holiness were only a matter of mental agility, then computers would be sacred.

Reaching for the heart in preaching is not mere pandering to audience frailties. Comprehensive communication of the Gospel must be based on a sound biblical understanding of human nature. Wayne Oates, professor of behavioral psychology at the University of Louisville School of Medicine, writes:

> The Hebrew-Christian understanding of personality is a holistic one. Jesus states the commandment which is "first of all": "Hear, O Israel, the Lord our God, the Lord is one; and you shall love the Lord your God with all your heart, and with all your soul, and with all your strength." The Greek word, "holes," is translated "all" and is repeated four times [in the passage]. My approach to understanding the human personality is to emphasize the oneness and totality rather than the division of personality into separate "faculties." When a person loves with all his or her mind, the whole being is involved, not just one part of the personality. Therefore, when you and I preach to the emotional needs of our audience, we are addressing them as total beings and not just as a "bundle of feelings."[1]

Even as formal an expositor as Jay Adams observes:

> To experience an event in preaching is to enter into that event so fully that the emotions appropriate to that event are felt, just as if one were actually going through it. When a preacher says what he relates in such a way that he stimulates one or more of the five senses, thus triggering emotion, then the listener may be said to "experience" the event. In that way, the event will become "real" to him, which means it has become concretized (or personalized), memorable, and, in the fullest sense of the word, understandable.[2]

Illustrations that engage the emotions address people the way the Bible does. Far from being unintellectual or unethical, illustrations that involve the whole person in the process of understanding operate in a manner consistent with the biblical concept of our complex nature. Questions such as, "What does this mean to me?" and, "How am I—how is my world—affected by this?" are in part answered by our emotions. Our feelings help explain to us (and to those to whom we express them) the impact of truths, events, and persons we confront. Illustrations that capture these feelings communicate Scripture in terms more reflective of reality than irrationality.

Sometimes preachers fear using illustrations because of their emotive features. When illustrations expand the emotional dimensions of a sermon, we may question whether truth can be carefully contained. The fear of emotionalism (i.e., the rule of the emotions over rationality) has a legitimate foundation. Many Christians fall into sin by allowing their hearts to rule over sound biblical principles. But emotions are not necessarily the antithesis of rationality. In fact, there is a certain irrationality in being unaffected by matters of vital importance to our lives and souls. It makes no sense *not* to feel anything when love, hate, pain, grief, joy, anger, or disappointment occur. Not to control emotions is wrong, but not to experience emotions is warped.

If one's emotions do not swell when reading Mary's praise in the Magnificat, then the Incarnation is not fully appreciated. A heart not rent by Christ's lament, "My God, my God, why have you forsaken me?" does not truly understand the Crucifixion. The heart and the mind must both contribute to our understanding for true comprehension. Scripture recognizes as much; sermons should reflect the same. Discarding illustrations because they appeal to the emotions neglects a path to understanding that Scripture itself endorses and follows.

Reaching the Will

When illustrations arouse emotions they do more than pass information on to the mind. They stimulate decision-making responses; they influence our will. We do not make decisions solely on the basis of what we know. We also decide because of how we feel about what we know. Illustrations recognize and employ this dynamic. Motivations for us to act in accordance with God's Word are frequently best forged in the illuminating fires of illustration.[3] When we become intellectually aware of what our emotions signal, decision-making necessarily results. We may choose to act on our emotions or to ignore them, but either course requires an engagement of the will.

Illustrations are therefore doors that preachers open to allow listeners to experience a concept; and by experiencing it, to understand it, interact with it, and act upon it. Illustrations that involve listeners in life-situation experiences express truths in the mode that comprehension, emotions, and decisions are most commonly and most powerfully galvanized. Preachers who reach listeners through this medium strengthen their communication, heighten comprehension, and foster spiritual change.

Consequently, instead of requiring an abandonment of the intellect, as some of the theories of preaching discussed in the previous chapter suggest, illustrations with emotive content force the mind into action. When a preacher elicits emotions through enabling a person to experience a life-situation illustration and at the same time dispenses sound teaching, rationality and resolve unite as powerful agents of change.[4]

THE PATTERN OF SCRIPTURE

Linking theoretical concepts to experience is vital, for neither learning nor communication occurs in isolation. We learn something new by discovering how it relates to what experience has already taught us, and the clearer the connection, the more thorough our understanding. Illustrations forge these connections by inviting us to make comparisons to our experiences or to empathize with those of others through narrative.

This, no doubt, is why the the Holy Spirit fills the Bible

with narrative accounts, poetic images, and symbols. Only a fraction of Scripture would remain if the "illustrative" components were removed.[5] Alister McGrath summarizes emphatically, *"Narrative is the main literary type found in Scripture. Indeed, some have even suggested that it is the only literary form in Scripture—an obvious, though perhaps understandable, exaggeration."*[6] The Bible does not exclude propositional statements, but their proportion is a fraction of the images and narratives.[7] The Spirit who inspires Scripture seems to echo the conclusion that people tend to grasp images more readily than propositions, but if they take hold of enough images, they can handle the propositions.[8]

In other words, the Lord supplies the metaphors by which he may be understood across time, distance, and culture.[9] By seeing God at work in the lives of those with whom we can identify, in a world we can know, we understand his nature and his requirements for us. By giving illustrations in Scripture, God not only provides the mechanism to be understood, but also anchors meaning so as not to be misunderstood. Preachers must follow this same pattern. They must unite deep feeling and lofty thoughts in their preaching, for these two complement each other.

Covenant Symbol

The Old Testament consistently weds propositional explanation and illustration. The communication style of Moses and the Prophets seems to imply that neither images nor statements may stand alone by themselves. Propositional summary and explanation are required to dress the meaning of illustrative material. Conversely, propositional truths are rarely left naked of illustrative clothing.

God uses pictures to explain even the most foundational theological concepts. The Tree of Life and the Tree of the Knowledge of Good and Evil symbolize the Adamic covenant (Gen. 2). God pledged the Noahic covenant with the visual token of a rainbow (Gen. 9). He sealed the Abrahamic covenant both with a traditional contractual ceremony (Gen. 15) and with a foreshadowing sign of bloodshed (Gen. 17). The Lord established the Mosaic covenant in signs and symbolic wonders (e.g., the burning bush, the staff turned into a snake, water turned to blood, and the Red Sea parted), maintained it in symbol and ceremony (e.g., the ark of the covenant, the scapegoat, the Paschal lamb, the entire temple economy, the phylacteries, and various feasts), and characterized its truths in symbol-laden narratives (e.g., the provision of manna, the bronze snake, wandering in the wilderness, and entry into Canaan—the Sabbath land).

Historical Narrative

Old Testament books of history (including the historical narratives of Moses) are just what their designation indicates—narrative upon narrative that reveal God's redemptive plan by characterizing his work in the history of the covenant people. These histories—including the accounts of Joshua, Gideon, Samson, Samuel, Saul, David, Solomon, and all the subsequent kings and prophets—do not contain much in the way of stated principles of systematic theology. God unveils his truth in narrative. The recounting of events that lead to the establishment of the Davidic covenant and Israel's subsequent history as it responds, rebels, and is restored, conveys the covenant promises and the covenant nature of our God. In all their details and personalities the histories are underscoring the central truth that "the LORD, the LORD, [is] the compassionate and gracious God, slow to anger, abounding in love and faithfulness, maintaining love to thousands, and forgiving wickedness, rebellion and sin. Yet he does not leave the guilty unpunished" (Ex. 34:6–7). The historical writers rarely state this proposition, but its truths are clearly explicated, easily understood, long remembered, and easily applied because of the stories that illustrate its essence.

Poetic Image

Biblical truths often find their most profound expression in the books of poetry, but here again the propositional statements are balanced with illustrative material. These wisdom books ordinarily do not contain formal narratives (Job is a notable exception), but by their very nature they abound in metaphor and example.

The parallel structure of Hebrew poetry makes virtually every phrase an analogy. This analogous structure accents the rich treasure of poetic images that communicate inspired thought. David describes the man of God as "a tree planted by streams of water" (Ps. 1:3). Picturing God's protection, the psalmist writes, "He will cover you with his feathers, and under his wings you will find refuge" (Ps. 91:4). The psalms variously describe God as a tabernacle, a rock, a refuge, a fortress, a king, a shepherd, etc.[10] When humans are out of communion with this God their unrepentant condition also receives experiential description. Spiritual despair can hardly be more vividly depicted than this: "When I kept silent, my bones wasted away through my groaning all the day long. For day and night your hand was heavy upon me; my strength was sapped as in the heat of summer" (Ps. 32:3–4). The examples of truths related through imagery and analogy from the poetic books are too numerous to list, of course, for their use is the very nature of poetry. It is enough to note here that in these Scriptures illustration and proposition kiss without complaint.

Prophetic Example

Despite the concentration of propositions in the prophetic books, illustrations remain significant. Among the many examples, God commands Jeremiah to hide a linen belt and retrieve it after many days. When he does retrieve the belt, it is ruined. The Lord says, "In the same way I will ruin the pride of Judah and the great pride of Jerusalem" (Jer. 13:9). Ezekiel gathers his belongings in open view to warn the people of Israel that they will be forced to pack for exile if they do not repent. "Perhaps they will understand, though they are a rebellious house," says the Lord (Ezek. 12:3).

Similar episodes appear in the minor prophets. God requires Hosea to keep forgiving and receiving his wife, Gomer, though she turns to adultery with others. God says, "Love her as the LORD loves the Israelites, though they turn to other gods. . ." (Hos. 3:1). On a contrasting note God shows the prophet Amos a basket of ripe fruit and says, "The time is ripe for my people Israel; I will spare them no longer" (Amos 8:2). The prophetic books, like the rest of the Old Testament, consistently communicate with metaphor, image, and analogy.

The Pattern of Jesus

A familiar hymn that speaks of Christ's life-pattern of instruction asks simply, "It is the way the Master went; should not the servant tread it still?" How did the Master communicate divine truths? The Scriptures say, "He did not say anything to them without using a parable" (Mark 4:34). Christ's motives for using this preaching device were multiple, of course, but he used it consistently.[11] He did not live in an "age of visual literacy," at least in terms of modern media, yet illustrations pervaded his preaching and teaching. If in his time illustrations were important, they are still vital today.

Christ actually followed a long-established pattern. His preaching most consistently reflects the pre-Christian rabbinic teaching form known as Haggadah (the way of story, as opposed to Halakah, the way of reasoned reflection on the Law).[12]

Illustrative techniques and principles that spell out salvation's story constantly beacon from the pages of the Gospels. According to Ian MacPherson, the parabolic element in Luke's gospel amounts to 52 percent of the total, while the illustrative content of all Jesus' recorded teaching is 75 percent.[13] These words of Jesus, comprising 20 percent of the New Testament (the rough equivalent of twelve sermons thirty minutes long)[14] yield significant evidence of the Lord's own preaching methods and priorities. Though our own traditions make it difficult, we should not ignore New Testament teaching and the practice in the primitive church in our New Testament preaching. At the same time, we should recognize that present emphases on developing "universal abstractions" and "hortatory accent with few examples" may reflect more the rhetoric of Greece and Rome than the speech of Jerusalem and Jesus.[15]

The Pauline Exception?

Some argue that Paul breaks the biblical pattern of coordinating experiential detail with propositional argument. Unquestionably the epistles of the New Testament in general, and of Paul in particular, concentrate on propositions. But the epistles do not undermine the use of illustration in preaching. An epistle is not a sermon. One who tries to establish homiletical models on epistolary forms is on shaky ground at best. When we do see Paul preaching in the New Testament he is hardly unconscious of the need for illustrative material in his messages. New Testament historian David Calhoun suggests that the chief differences among the four Pauline sermons to unbelievers in the book of Acts are the allusions Paul chooses to relate to the four different cultures represented by the separate audiences.[16]

Those who claim a Pauline exception to the biblical practice of illustration actually ignore much of Paul. Even in his most doctrinal passages the apostle liberally sprinkles allusions to the narrative history of Israel, the arena, the sports field, the military, the marketplace, the temple, the home, the school, and more.[17] Paul is not nearly so ready a witness for the prosecution of illustrations as a cursory investigation might indicate. Serious cross-examination of his own testimony may reveal that the apostle has a similar modus operandi.

Not so obvious as Paul's own use of illustrative material is God's use of illustrative material to clarify Paul. After all, were it not for the narratives of Acts, many of the references, comments, and arguments of Paul would be oblique at best. With the Lukan travelogue we have a ready-made experiential context for much of the argumentation Paul offers. Without the divine strategy of providing Acts as an illustrative guide, Paul's propositions might prove impossible to navigate.

The Incarnate Illustration

The truths God most carefully embodied for our understanding confirm the importance of the biblical pattern of illustration. In a very real sense our knowledge and perception of God is a product of the most explicit illustration of his nature—Jesus Christ, the Incarnate Word. The glory of God, which cannot be seen, was revealed in the Son who made known the Father (cf. John 1:14, 18). The Greek word for "made known" traditionally means "to draw out in narrative."[18] In other words, the stories of Christ's life actually illustrate the nature of the heavenly Father. Jesus is the Word *about* God, as well as the Word *from* God. Doctrinal propositions do not predominate in the narratives of the Gospels (though they are certainly evident on occasion). The life of Christ chiefly illumines the divine nature in the Gospels. Narrative becomes God's chief vehicle for our comprehension of the spiritual. Concrete events and real persons interacting with each other disclose and clarify the divine. God's method of using the Divine Illustration along with doctrinal statement in the communication of redemption's greatest truth emphasizes how essential both elements are for our understanding.

The apostle John presents Christ as the archetypal illustration of the divine nature with words almost startling in their reflection of the role that experience plays in understanding:

> That which was from the beginning, which we have heard, which we have seen with our eyes, which we have looked at and our hands have touched—this we proclaim concerning the word of life. The life appeared; we have seen it and testify to it, and we proclaim to you that eternal life, which was with the Father and has appeared to us. We proclaim to you what we have seen and

heard, so that you also may have fellowship with us. And our fellowship is with the Father and with his Son, Jesus Christ (1 John 1:1–3).

John helps us understand Scripture's most wonderful and most mysterious truth by grounding our perception in statements involving our senses. But as instructive as this technique is, the results are even more critical. By re-creating this sensory experience for us, John says we may share in his spiritual fellowship. His description is the door through which we enter to participate in the relationship he already shares with the Father. There can be no better argument for using illustrations to present life-situation experiences that clarify and disclose biblical truths. When preachers do as much, they not only better inform their listeners, but they also open an experiential door through which those listeners must pass to know the Father and his Son.

ON THE PATH OF SCRIPTURE

The best preachers want to persuade people by the truths of the Gospel, not by homiletical tricks. Concern that illustrations may lead on extrabiblical escapades reflects a healthy regard for the unique authority of God's Word. But any outline, any argument, any nuance, any sentence that is not directly off the pages of Scripture, in the order of Scripture, and of the length of the original Scripture, in some way introduces human interpolation. If we are to preach rather than simply quote the Bible at length, such invention is necessary. We should not reject illustrations just because they do not have a verse reference. Illustrations have the imprimatur of divine precedent and the sanction of the Spirit who inspired the Word.

For reasons that will become increasingly clear, the Bible enhances propositional statements with experiential data, identifiable examples, and memorable images. Now the question is whether sermons that ignore the structure of Scripture are truly on the same path as their inspired guide. Is only the content of

Scripture normative, or is not the form of Scripture itself instructive?[19] Those who would follow Scripture in practice as well as in content should take note of both its patterns and methods of reasoning. The result will be sermons that reflect a greater respect for the wisdom of Scripture's structure and a greater loyalty to Scripture's form.

The Spirit who once gave a fallen world inspired words now speaks through preaching to minds that are just as much in need. If the Spirit of God found illustration useful in the Word to be honored for endless ages, we should consider well how we can use such a tool today. The Spirit who inspired Holy Writ can guard the preaching of those whose minds are set on him so that their illustrations do not become barriers to truth, but rather become bridges to the Gospel.

Notes

1. Wayne E. Oates, "Preaching to Emotional Needs," *Preaching* 1, 5 (1986), p. 5.
2. Jay E. Adams, *Preaching with Purpose* (Grand Rapids: Baker, 1982), p. 86.
3. Thomas A. Ringness, *The Affective Domain in Education* (Boston: Little, Brown and Co., 1975), p. 43.
4. Elaine Batcher, *Emotion in the Classroom*, Praeger Studies in Ethnographic Perspectives on American Education, ed. Ray C. Rist (New York: Praeger, 1981), p. 151.
5. Ralph Lewis, "The Triple Brain Test of a Sermon," *Preaching* 1, 2 (1985), p. 10.
6. Alister E. McGrath, "The Biography of God," *Christianity Today* 35 (July 22, 1991), p. 23.
7. Henry Grady Davis, *Design for Preaching* (Philadelphia: Fortress, 1958), p. 157.
8. Ian MacPherson, *The Art of Illustrating Sermons* (Nashville: Abingdon, 1964), p. 40.
9. John W. Sanderson, *Mirrors of His Glory* (Phillipsburg, N.J.: Presbyterian and Reformed, 1991), pp. vii–viii.
10. Ibid., pp. 3ff.
11. For a discussion of Mark 4:10–12, the passage in which Jesus tells why he used parables, see below, pp. 129–30.
12. Belden C. Lane, "Rabbinical Stories: A Primer on Theological Method," *The Christian Century* 98 (1981), p. 1306.

13. MacPherson, *The Art of Illustrating Sermons*, p. 40.
14. Lewis, "Triple Brain Test," p. 11.
15. Ibid.
16. Personal interview with Dr. David Calhoun, associate professor of church history at Covenant Theological Seminary in St. Louis, April 24, 1986.
17 Thomas V. Liske, *Effective Preaching* (New York: Macmillan, 1960), p. 185.
18. "Made known" is the first aorist (effective) middle indicative of *exēgeomai*, cf. A. T. Robertson, *Word Pictures in the New Testament* (Nashville: Broadman, 1932), p. 18.
19. See the excellent discussion of this question in Don M. Wardlaw's *Preaching Biblically: Creating Sermons in the Shape of Scripture* (Philadelphia: Westminster, 1983), pp. 11–25.

Chapter 3

Insights from Learning and Communication Theories

When Ilion Jones stated, "Illustrations are essential because of the way the human mind functions,"[1] we did not
know as much about the mind as we do now. But a half-century
of research confirms he was right on target. The "way the
human mind functions" to make what is foreign, familiar—to
make the abstract, real—is by integrating the rational with the
experiential. We understand truth when we observe it in the
context of a human situation. Illustrations provide the mechanism for this life-specific understanding and are thus indispensable to effective preaching. This conclusion is confirmed
through an analysis of numerous learning and communication
theories.

THE DISCORDANT SYMPHONY
OF LEARNING THEORIES

It is beyond the scope of this book to examine all the
theories exploring how we perceive and think. Many modern

researchers write from perspectives that are unbiblical or even explicitly anti-Christian. However, a brief look at some significant theories is worthwhile as background to further biblical study. Note that despite their varying philosophies, all these theorists link learning (variously defined) to experience.

Reward Theories

Learning theory for some researchers has its origins in the work of Ivan Petrovich Pavlov. Pavlovian conditioning repeatedly pairs an unconditioned stimulus (e.g., food) with a conditioned stimulus (e.g., a bell) until the conditioned stimulus alone elicits a conditioned response (e.g., salivation). This scheme was later inverted in the "operant conditioning" approach developed by B. F. Skinner, in which reward is conditional upon an anticipated response. Both variations see learning progressing because prior experiences are habituated or recalled in response to current needs.

Reward/response theories have almost become a "given" in learning philosophies because they show up in so many experimental models. The "given" may be obscured by the variety and complexity of later designs and theories, but this constant always beacons: experience is the lens of learning.

Mapping Theories

Edward Lee Thorndike challenges the determinism of some reward theories, but he also tries to show that experience instructs far more than pure logical insight. Some of Thorndike's "laws" are particularly important for homiletical consideration:

Set (attitude). The change made in a learner depends upon the mental set brought into the learning situation.

Response by Analogy (Identical Elements). Response to a situation is similar to responses to previously experienced related situations. Amount of transfer between situations is determined by the number of common elements.

Prepotency. Response to the environments is selective and determined by what elements we attend to. Those elements that are more prominent will be responded to more readily.[2]

Edwin Ray Guthrie's one law of learning summarizes Thorndike and crystallizes a useful thought: "What is done in a given situation depends on what was previously done in the same situation."[3] While the conclusion is too stronge as far as learning through preaching is concerned, since it leaves out the superseding work of the Holy Spirit, still, for ordinary types of learning it is important to understand that the mind recognizes, organizes, and orders by comparing present matters with past experience.

Edward Chace Tolman disagrees with the reward theorists, claiming that any significant mental or physical response adds features to the sensory "map" that the mind creates to discover what things mean. We understand ideas and concepts by identifying where they are located on this map constructed of our previous experiences. We can link this conclusion with Steinaker and Bell's discovery that vicarious as well as actual experiences are effective for learning purposes. Preachers communicate with greatest impact when a response-inducing experience (actual or vicarious) accompanies their words.

Context Theories

The Gestalt theorists, while arguing that learning often occurs with a sudden feeling of understanding—an insight— nonetheless say this insight "requires [that] certain aspects be seen in relation to one another, that they appear as a single gestalt [i.e., integrated structure]."[4] Experience must commingle with the present in order for an insight to "make sense." Kurt Lewin's "life space" theory is explicitly experiential. He argues all behavior, conscious or unconscious, is determined by the effect of stimuli on an individual's goals, motives, hindrances, etc., that constitute his life space.

Of particular note to preachers is Robert Gagne's analysis of attitude learning. Gagne says that certain motor skills must develop as the mind matures before an attitude can be learned. Before we can mentally understand some matters, we must experience appropriate physical responses. Gagne adds that because of the limitations of verbal statements, a respected model must sometimes demonstrate an attitude before another can learn the attitude. In other words, an attitude must be embodied by someone for it to be comprehended. Illustrations that depict individuals reflecting desired attitudes give listeners hope of acquiring those attitudes. No wonder the Bible uses so many personal accounts.

Computer Theories

Attitude change is far more important to most pastors than merely giving out information, but the latter has its place. Spiritually responsible behavior must be informed. Though they tend to be disturbingly mechanistic, "information processing" theorists give insights into how we get usable facts into our heads. Their computations reveal that the data base that accesses and interprets new information is experience. Robert Wyer writes:

> Each processor is capable of receiving information, operating upon it according to certain rules, storing the results of these operations in memory, altering the contents of certain areas of memory to which new information is relevant, and ultimately reporting the results of these operations in a form that is implicitly or explicitly specified by a "user."[5]

It is difficult to determine whether Wyer is describing a human being or a machine. However, his learning model has important implications for preaching. For a person to process information it is not enough that the information simply be presented. The information must be integrated into the matrix

of preexisting stimuli, memory features, and operative procedures that characterize the "receiver." In short, the information
must be processed through a person's experiential background.
In the preaching situation, illustrations call this experiential
background to the listener's mind.

Learning Theories in Concert

The learning theorists could hardly be more philosophi-
cally diverse: Pavlovians battle operant conditionists; progres-
sive and sequential learning theorists contrast with single-trial
theorists; idealistic goal-directed behaviorists must coexist with
pragmatic information processors. Yet from this discordant
symphony there emerges one consistent note: the experiential
world is the context, if not the very medium, of our understanding. What I experience through my senses, my emotions,
or the recall of them is the framework on which I build
comprehension and through which I interpret new information. Therefore, to explain propositions, principles, or concepts
through materials keyed to lived-body experiences is not only
entertaining but essential.

THE HARMONY OF COMMUNICATION THEORIES

In addition to learning theories, the need to ground
understanding in experience also echoes through the theories
of communication in an array of catch phrases. Advocates say
we communicate best when we couch ideas in "human interest
accounts";[6] "life-situations";[7] "life-stories";[8] "experience-
centered messages";[9] "narrative paradigms";[10] "firsthand encounter";[11] "piece of life illustrations";[12] "lived-body experience";[13] and even "a story that participates in the stories of
those who have lived, who live now, and who will live in the
future."[14] The variety of terms grants rich expression to the
power of personal experience. We understand what is real to
us. When an experience touches us or when we sense the

impact it could have upon us, then and only then, can we comprehend it fully.

The linkage of knowing and doing—of understanding and experience—strengthens as this century progresses. In the early 1950s Edgar Dale demonstrated that learning occurs most effectively through direct, purposeful involvement. Teachers trained in the 1960s pondered implications of a "learning pyramid" that showed we learn 10 percent of what we hear, 30 percent of what we see, but 60 percent of what we do. By the 1970s researchers could rank types of experiences that most effectively teach and, in doing so, discovered that people learn as much from "fully described" experiences as they do from actual experiences.[15] That discovery underscores the important of narrative in all forms of communication.

Listeners who experience concepts—even vicariously— actually know more than those who must consider words and ideas in the abstract. What preachers have intuited for generations has a solid scientific foundation. Meaningful thought grows best when rooted in a perceived situation.[16] This discovery discloses the hidden value of illustrations. Listeners simply understand more when messages exhibit spiritual truths in stories of identifiable experiences.

Furthermore, communication on an experiential level enables the listener to move quickly from a level of knowing to a level of doing. Personal reflection on any subject becomes meaningful when "I think" is converted to "I am able to." The idea is contextualized in the experience that makes the concept applicable to the life of the listener, and the idea's import is predicted in the context of experiential dynamics before it can be truly meaningful to that individual.[17] Real communication does not occur until a speaker and listener contextualize words in like fields of experience. The former predicates meaning based upon his or her field of experience, the latter predicts meaning based upon his or her field of experience. Any narrative mechanism, such as illustration, that readily defines these fields of experience for both parties, makes communication possible.[18]

In sum, it is primarily through *narrative* that captures, defines, and describes experience that we create meaning for ourselves and others. Walter Fisher insists that narrative is not just another communication device; rather, it is "the master metaphor." It subsumes all other communication models and methods.[19] Narratives, especially as used in life-situations illustrations, enable us to know who we are, what others communicate, and what God communicates. They make it possible for us as preachers to bridge the gap between our present century and the world of the Bible, as well as the gap between the pulpit and the pew.

ECHOES IN CULTURE

While not a learning or communication theory as such, the present-day "age of visual literacy"[20] also suggests why preachers must listen to the modern researchers whose work underscores the need for vivid illustrations. The average adult who spends fifty hours a year in a pew will also spend two thousand hours at home watching television. The average school child will spend more hours in the TV room than in a classroom.[21] Some estimate that average American children will spend more time watching television before entering school than they will listen to their parents in their lifetime. Add to these influences the entertainments of movies and video arcades; the visual bombardments of highway advertisements and grocery aisle packaging; and the educational shift to overhead projectors, video tape classes, analog computers— the conclusion is inescapable: "Ours is par excellence the Age of Illustration, an age when people are habituated to picture thinking."[22]

Distaste for words divorced from experience typifies our whole culture. Schools are turning more and more from lecture-teaching to involvement-teaching. Studies indicate that 70 percent of students of all ages are not analytic learners. Eight or nine out of every ten junior high students engage in problem solving without linear reasoning. Six of ten high school students learn better through exposure to concrete experiences rather than by being led through abstract thought.[23]

The case study method so typical of traditional law schools now dominates many forms of professional training. Business professionals now expect the weekend seminars they attend to involve them in the examination of numerous "case studies," whether they are being taught how to sell tax-free bonds or negotiate a labor contract. Back at the office on Monday, these same professionals will instinctively evaluate the success of the seminar based on how realistic and down-to-earth were the sample situations presented. The accrediting agencies of the nation's major colleges and universities are now providing funding for training veteran teachers in all major disciplines to teach with case study methods. The message is clear: involve students or they will not learn. Principles without particulars will not be grasped or retained.

In a similar vein, the average person in the pew simply does not depend on words and propositions alone for information. If the nation goes to war, anticipates election news, or craves information on a tragedy, printed words and expert analysts are not the primary informants. The modern mental palate lusts for the sights and sounds of battle more than it wants statistical analysis. Crowds in malls and airports gather around TV monitors waiting for the slightest glimpse of new material while newspapers brimming with analysis lie in stacks at neighboring newsstands. The newspapers will not all go unread. A few persons depend primarily on newspapers or news magazines, and many more use printed sources to get more details. But even the news publishers know that only 4 or 5 percent of their customers will read beyond the first paragraph of the average story, and that readership will treble or quadruple with any story bearing a picture—with the caption being the most read paragraph of the entire account. Audience interest and information consumption increase with sensory involvement even in these media.

Some believe these trends result from modern culture's audio-visual addictions. Televisions and stereos have become the sensory wallpaper of many an American's daily existence. Electronic sights and sounds accompany every thought and waking moment. Computer software companies and cassette tape publishers bank on our need for sensory input by marketing interactive learning programs in *TV Guide* and on airline flight magazines. Whether these trends are actually a result of recent cultural developments or are the exploitation of more basic human thought processes remains a question. But there is no question that our culture trains us to reason and react experientially.

Contemporary preachers must acknowledge these cultural challenges, even if they are unsure how much to accommodate them. While we should not too hastily abandon our rich preaching heritage, we must ask how we can best serve present needs. Preaching practices that ignore the importance of experiential discovery simply indicate insensitivity to the typical parishioner's daily life and learning.

APPLYING THE THEORIES

In the face of these cultural changes, the conclusions of learning and communication theorists do much to indicate why illustrations are so important. Beyond their much-cited ability to garner attention, provide nonredundant repetition, and sustain sermon interest, illustrations create experiential dynamics that actually further understanding, thus helping people change as well as listen. Modern theorists are only helping us understand principles long observed and employed by the ablest of communicators. Ilion T. Jones writes:

> Unquestionably, Jesus chose deliberately to use a method of teaching that bypassed the necessity of this [propositional] definition of terms, for he neither defined terms nor attempted to prove the truth with close-knit arguments. He took a short cut to the minds of his hearers. He taught in concrete rather than abstract terms. He certainly never heard of the modern psychological term "apperception" but nevertheless understood the mental processes which that term describes, namely: that people

interpret what they hear and see in terms of what they already know. If they possess no knowledge with which to interpret new ideas, no communication of those ideas can take place.[24]

Jones goes too far. Jesus did define terms, and he did occasionally teach in abstractions. The point is well taken, however, that Jesus linked his teachings to concrete experiential materials.[25]

Linking Learning and Preaching

John Killinger specifically uses learning theories to justify sermon illustrations. After citing traditional reasons why preachers use illustrations, Killinger uses an old quotation to point in a new direction:

> *Illustrations relate theology to life.* As Sangster says, they "earth" a sermon. They take it out of the realm of abstraction and anchor it to everyday occurrences, to the things people know. . . . Illustrations are where the sermon puts on its overalls and goes to work in people's lives. The people in the congregation know in the illustrations whether the sermon is practical or not; if they can see the principles at work in the stories, then they know the principles will work for them.[26]

Killinger's words harmonize with those of other instructors who sense the connections between modern learning theorists' focus on experience and the structures of preaching.

If experience secures the comprehension of one's world and others' words, then communication tools that use experiential dynamics are indispensable. Here is where illustrations furnish vital service to sermons. We can know a biblical truth intuitively or logically but fail to understand it emotionally, psychologically, or spiritually by guarding ourselves from the experiencing of the truth. Illustrations preclude such evasion. Listeners who enter the narrative world of an illustration vicariously *are* involved in the life experience that helps disclose a truth's full meaning.[27]

Integrating Thought and Understanding

Simply because a concept has been formulated into propositional statements for rational consideration does not mean it can be fully apprehended. Truth principles remain personally opaque if they do not coincide with one's world. If I have no reference for a concept, I cannot understand it.[28] This is true whether one is speaking about the horrors of the Great Depression or the comfort of trusting God when a loved one dies. Both concepts can be explained propositionally without being understood fully. Real understanding requires the dynamic of "being there." Common sense affirms that there is greater understanding with more experience. What modern research offers is the relatively new argument that, without lived-body experience, matters to be comprehended—even words—cannot be fully understood.[29]

Employing Perception

Just as the psychological is never independent of the physiological, the rational is inextricably linked to the physical. Against traditional learning dualisms that separate the functions of body and mind, contemporary theorists posit a holistic "existence" that teaches by the involvement of body and mind—the whole person—in experience.[30] Personal encounter provides the "mirror" in which everything that one confronts must be seen in order for what is perceived to be understood. Thus, the perception of anything requires the lived-body experiencing of it, not just to collect sense data (how it tastes, smells, looks, feels, etc.), but to focus and orient consciousness that makes sensation, contextualization, and understanding possible.

If the theorists are correct, then a full understanding of those matters deepest in the human heart is tied to lived-body experience. Preachers have long argued that there is a significant difference between head knowledge and heart knowledge, between informing the mind and informing the whole person. Perhaps today's researchers are providing insight into how truly great these differences are. These conclusions add significance and vividness to Killinger's assessment of the usefulness of illustrations. He says:

> **Personal Illustrations.** These are the ones, I confess, that I like best. Stories from men's and women's experiences, from children's experiences, narrated by the persons they happened to, shared by the preacher. There is a warmth about them that makes them very appealing. They give an honest ring to the gospel that does not come from anything else. They make the gospel seem real, touchable, truly incarnate.[31]

Illustrations' link to experience can make the Gospel real, fleshly, and interpretable. Therefore, to explain propositions, principles, or concepts through illustrative materials keyed to lived-body experiences would not seem to be side-tracked communication, but full-fledged communication.

Choreographing Meaning

The notion that illustrations are simplistic concessions to popular expectations is not only at odds with modern learning and communication theories, it contradicts the experience of most preachers. What minister has not discovered the ease with which an expositional truth can be propositionally stated, only to agonize for hours how to illustrate that truth in a moving, relevant fashion? The findings of the learning theorists may help explain why the process is so difficult. In order to relate truths experientially, the preacher must himself delve to that level of being where mind, soul, body, world, and psyche are real. Until he has done so—until he has plumbed the depths of his emotions, relationships, and experiences and integrated what he discovers in those oceans with what he knows intellectually—his own understanding is not complete.

But to seek such a complete understanding—that is, to depart from the abstract and uncover the concrete in the difficult and sometimes treacherous realities of self, other, and world—is the most rigorous of homiletical tasks. The preacher must travel an intellectual "second mile" to create illustrations that fulfill their potential. It is not a mark of intellectual capitulation to use illustrations. It may well be a sign of intellectual sloth and communication resignation not to use them.

Illustration requires preachers to think about what can be heard as well as what can be said. They must do a sort of "double-think." Preachers must first think on what a passage means to them, and then they must think of what will communicate that meaning to the persons for whom God has made them responsible. In other words, they must journey through the lives and experiences of others as well as search their own souls. It is hard, grueling, sacrificial work, which may be precisely why illustrations are so often shunned under the guise of erudition.

Discovering Artifacts

Individuals with significantly different lived-body experiences have trouble understanding each other. This simple observation leads to consideration of a final, significant contribution of contemporary communication theory. If preacher and parishioner do share understanding, it is because their experience interlocks in some way. Units of experience they share translate words and concepts for each of them.[32] Thus, events sliced from life hold powerful communication potential. The power can be harnessed.

In the terms of communication research, an event that one calls to mind in order to make sense of an idea is an "artifact" of experience. Much as archaeologists excavate artifacts from mounds of sediment to interpret an ancient culture for contemporaries, listeners unearth experiences from layers of consciousness to interpret ideas for present understanding. These artifacts of experience may be resurrected from deep layers of consciousness or may only have been recently deposited by a preacher. Still, whether the artifact is new or old, it retains the power necessary to give meaning to words and phrases that surround it.

But what is the precise nature of this artifact that is used to interpret surrounding concepts? The artifact is actually a unit of experience that "typifies" for the listener what the preacher is saying.[33] The experience is lifted out of its setting with its essential elements frozen into some recognizable form so that it can act as an object of comparison for the words, phrases, and concepts in present experience. In written or spoken form, the sliced-out experience takes the form of a narrative. An experience that has been marked by a beginning and an end, that has progression of action and thought between these points, and that can be called to consciousness from memory, is a story. This understanding grounds the thinking behind the current explosion of interest in narrative theory. Because narratives provide the contexts needed for individual understanding and can be readily shared between individuals, stories provide both the experiential and relational resources needed for highly effective communication.

SYNCHRONIZING KNOWING AND DOING

Educational research in the twentieth century, while frequently flawed from a spiritual perspective, clearly demonstrates that comprehensive understanding that leads to informed decision-making and responsible action is more than a purely cognitive process. A friend of mine who recruits physicians for medical centers explains how he knows this real-life truth. When a hospital, medical firm, or town needs a physician with specialized talents, my recruiter friend tries to find a qualified doctor and encourages him to move to the place of need. Often there is much competition for the services of such doctors and much reluctance on their part to make such a move. My friend and other recruiters in his company, therefore, have the job of not only informing, but of persuading. It is not an easy task.

One must learn much about human nature to be successful

in this business of motivating top professionals to make major moves. My friend says that he and other more experienced recruiters often smile knowingly at one another across a conference table when a new recruiter shares his frustrations about a particular doctor's unwillingness to make a move despite obvious advantages for all concerned.

A young recruiter may say about a doctor, "I don't understand why he is not responding. He knows the pay is better. The chances for career advancement are better. It's even a nicer town. He tells me he knows it's a better opportunity than what he has and, still, he won't commit himself."

The more experienced recruiters realize that decisions are not made simply on the basis of what one knows intellectually. As my more experienced friend says:

> The doctor cannot yet see himself in the new role. Intellectually he may know something is better for him, but he has no emotional commitment to the decision that has to be made. He cannot make such a decision until his heart and his head connect so that he can experience what his new position would mean for him and his family at an experiential as well as an intellectual level. New recruiters often supply the data necessary for a mental decision, but not the support necessary for an emotional commitment—and that is doing only half the job. Doing half the job doesn't get the job done in this business. We have to supply the experiences that help a doctor to see himself in the new practice so that he can transfer his intellectual knowledge into personal commitment.

For physician recruiters, supplying the experiences necessary to help a doctor make a major decision means taking the doctor to the town, introducing him to the people with whom he will be working, showing him the facilities, and proving the quality of the community in which he will be living. A doctor must experience the effects of his decision before he can be motivated to action. For preachers this is an important lesson. People do not make decisions simply because they are intellectually informed. No one has a true understanding of what they are being asked to do until they have the experiential data to evaluate the significance of the change being demanded. Because life-situation illustrations provide this experiential data, allowing individuals to "live through" the implications of their spiritual choices, they well serve life-changing preaching.

To sum up, human understanding in its fullest sense involves the will as well as the intellect, the heart as well as the mind, emotion as well as cognition, obedience as well as scholarship, and experience as well as erudition. Persons who make decisions without this full understanding are, in some degree, acting in ignorance even if their decisions are strictly rational. The truth that is most fully experienced is the truth that can be most responsibly acted upon. A preacher should be able to tell people to get ready, to get set, and to go where God commands because they have already been there in the illustrations of the message. The path that is already familiar to them is the one they are most likely to take.

Notes

1. Ilion T. Jones, *Principles and Practice of Preaching* (New York: Abingdon, 1956), p. 136.
2. For concise synopses of key developments in learning theory related to the experiential, I am much indebted to Byron Val Johnson, "A Media Selection Model for Use With a Homiletical Taxonomy" (Ph.D. diss.; Cardondale: Southern Illinois University, 1982), pp. 158–59.
3. Ibid, p. 164.
4. Ibid., p. 168 (for following discussion, see also pp. 169–73).
5. Ibid., p. 177.
6. The standard journalistic definition of "human interest accounts" allows that they are stories in which persons recognize things that have happened to them or could happen to them.
7. Lloyd M. Perry and Charles M. Sell provide an excellent discussion of the preachers and authors who use "life-situation" terminology in their book, *Speaking to Life's Problems* (Chicago: Moody Press, 1983), pp. 15–18.
8. Edmund A. Steimle, Morris J. Niedenthal, and Charles Rice, eds., *Preaching the Story* (Philadelphia: Fortress, 1980), p. 12. See also Rolf von Eckartsberg, "The Eco-Psychology of Personal Culture Building: An Existential Hermeneutic Approach," *Duquesne Stud-*

ies in Phenomenological Psychology, ed. Amadeo Giorgi, Richard Knowles, David L. Smith III (Atlantic Highlands, N.J.: Humanitas Press/Duquesne University Press, 1979), p. 233.

9. Ralph L. Lewis with Gregg Lewis, *Inductive Preaching: Helping People Listen* (Westchester, Ill.: Crossway, 1983), p. 41.

10. Walter R. Fisher, "Narration as a Human Communication Paradigm: The Case of Public Moral Argument," *Communication Monographs*, 51 (1984), p. 488. See also the subsequent article by Fisher, "The Narrative Paradigm: An Elaboration," *Communication Monographs*, 52 (1985), pp. 347–67.

11. Webb B. Garrison, *Creative Imagination in Preaching* (Nashville: Abingdon, 1960), pp. 95–96.

12. Louis Paul Lehman, *Put a Door on It* (Grand Rapids: Kregel, 1975), p. 27.

13. For Maurice Merleau-Ponty's particularly helpful notion of the "lived-body" and its function in our understanding the world, see his *Phenomenology of Perception*, trans. Colin Smith with revisions by Forrest Williams (London, 1962; rpt., Atlantic Highlands, N.J.: Humanities Press, 1981), pp. 274, 235–38, 383).

14. Fisher, "Narration as a Human Communication Paradigm," p. 6.

15. Johnson, "A Media Selection Model," p. 197; Norman Steinaker and Robert M. Bell, "A Proposed Taxonomy of Educational Objectives: The Experiential Domain," *Educational Technology* 15 (January 1975), pp. 15–16.

16. Merleau-Ponty, *Phenomenology of Perception*, p. 235.

17. Richard L. Lanigan, "Communication Models in Philosophy: Review and Commentary," in *International Communication Association Yearbook*, ed. Dan Nimmo, 3 (New Brunswick: Transaction Books, 1979), pp. 39–40.

18. For a more extensive analysis of numerous other communication theories and their interrelationship with modern uses of narrative, see the appendix to this book.

19. Walter Fisher, "Narration as a Human Communication Paradigm," p. 6.

20. See chapter 1, note 6.

21. Ibid., p. 11.

22. Ian MacPherson, *The Art of Illustrating Sermons* (Nashville: Abingdon, 1964), p. 39.

23. Lewis, *Inductive Preaching*, p. 10.

24. Jones, *Principles and Practice of Preaching*, p. 136.

25. Timothy K. Jones, "Reading Life Backwards," *Christianity Today* 33 (September 22, 1989), pp. 29–31.

26. John Killinger, *Fundamentals of Preaching* (Philadelphia: Fortress, 1985), p. 108.

27. For an excellent discussion of the role of experience in developing spiritual understanding as it is addressed in Calvinistic, Puritan, and Reformed theological history, see Klaas Runia, "Experience in the Reformed Tradition," *Theological Forum* of the Reformed Ecumenical Synod, 15, nos. 2 and 3 (April 1987), pp. 7–13. Runia places in proper perspective much of contemporary secular thought by demonstrating how "experience does not precede the Word but rather follows it." Encapsulating Calvin's thought, Runia explains, "Experience, however, is not a source of knowledge, in addition to Scripture. It is not an independent road to God, next to the revelation given in Scripture." Experience "functions as a hermeneutical key for the understanding of Scripture," which Runia and the Reformers make quite clear is not rooted in, nor limited by, human experience. Objective truth transcends human subjectivity, but full understanding of the Word of God, when opened by the Holy Spirit, is still contextualized for reflection and obedience by the experiential.

28. Maurice Merleau-Ponty, *The Phenomenology of Perception*, p. xix.

29. Ibid., pp. 239–40.

30. Ibid., p. 122, note.

31. Killinger, *Fundamentals of Preaching*, p. 118.

32. Richard Lanigan, "Phenomenology," *Encyclopedic Dictionary of Semiotics*, vol. 2, ed. Thomas Sebeok (Berlin: de Gruyter, 1987), pp. 564–67.

33. Alfred Schutz, *The Phenomenology of the Social World*, trans. George Walsh and Frederick Lehnert; Northwestern University Studies in Phenomenology and Existential Philosophy, gen. ed. John Wild (Evanston, Ill.: Northwestern University Press, 1967), p. 187.

Chapter 4

The Genius of Life-Situation Illustrations

WHY BE ENTHUSIASTIC ABOUT ILLUSTRATIONS?

Preachers who can see what illustrations do for preaching continue to advance their cause. Unfortunately, these advocates often describe what illustrations do, rather than determine why illustrations are necessary. Such pragmatic observations do little to disabuse those critics who maintain that illustrations are for feeble minds and shallow preachers. How should contemporary preachers determine the value of illustrations?

The Wrong Reasons

As late as 1964, Ian MacPherson claimed to have determined the importance of illustration by reading "all" the books written on the subject—they numbered six.[1] Such a meager canon hardly connotes a subject of great significance or value.
More helpful is W. E. Sangster's much reprinted and often

quoted *The Craft of Sermon Illustration*. Sangster cites seven uses for illustrations:

(1) They make the message clear. (2) They ease a congregation. (3) They make the truth impressive. (4) They make preaching interesting. (5) They make sermons remembered. (6) They help to persuade people. (7) They make repetition possible without weariness.[2]

Subsequent books on illustrations reiterate this list time and again. Unfortunately, some use the list negatively, implying that one must illustrate because of congregational limitations. Its members apparently cannot pay attention, give interest, or retain information without the spoon-feeding of an agreeable and sycophantic preacher.

The argument that preachers must pander to congregational deficiencies by illustrating reinforces the notion that illustrations are a necessary evil in preaching. Such a rationale may keep the books, card files, and microfiche catalogues of homiletical illustrations selling, but it will further convince conscientious pastors that illustrations are the charms of lower caste preachers.

The Right Reasons

There are better reasons to value illustrations. Earlier this century Dawson C. Bryan hinted at these as he explored previously uncharted territory. Bryan argued that listeners more typically make decisions based on "visual realization" rather than verbal argumentation.[3] This bold claim challenged older notions that illustrations simply make sermons more "pleasurable," "interesting," or "simplistic."[4] Bryan believed illustrations have unique explanatory and motivational powers. He understood that illustrations help audiences listen, but he also wanted to prove illustrations transform thought and actions. Sadly, at this point the scholar's reach exceeded his grasp. Communication studies had not sufficiently advanced to allow him to validate his claims.

Our analysis has confirmed what Bryan intuited. Illustrations do more than simply adorn thought. They persuade, they motivate, they stir the will, they touch the heart, they explain, and they cause decision-making. In this chapter we explore in some detail the value of using life-situation illustrations in preaching, thus vindicating a preacher's use of them and underscoring the beauty of the Lord's own communication choices in Scripture. Readers will discover that the Bible not only informs the practice of illustrating; illustration provides new ways to understand the wisdom of Scripture.

ESTABLISHING MEANING THROUGH NARRATIVE

The communication task God must perform through Scripture magnifies the importance of narrative for preaching. If, as noted in the previous chapter, even rudimentary human expressions require a background of shared stories to convey meanings effectively across distances and differences between persons, then the biblical text's dependence on narrative can hardly be overestimated. For believers to appropriate and apply eternal intentions today, Scripture must communicate transcendent expressions of eternal truth across cultural millennia to reach countless millions "from every nation, tribe, people, and language" (Rev. 7:9). Narrative makes the task possible. Through the stories of Scripture, narratives provide a clarifying sign system essential for communicating biblical propositions.

The verbal components of biblical statements are continually veiled and increasingly obscured by time, distance, and societal differences. Propositions alone cannot transmit meanings across the perception gaps that Scripture must bridge. Stories help eternal truths span centuries and cultures. Narratives frame needed propositions in an experiential context that provides reference for their verbal content, even as the propositions provide conceptual and linguistic material that allow the narratives to take shape. The narratives would have no structure without propositions, but the propositions would have no consistent meaning without narrative. Scripture's methodical use of both proposition and narrative underscores its sensitivity and reveals its genius. John Killinger writes:

> The Bible has this kind of balance about it. It is image and story, as we have said, but it is also law and history and proverb and philosophy. It alternates between these, so that story is always given a rational "spine" and statement is always provided a nearby illustration.[5]

Nowhere do the biblical writers assume that propositional statements alone will bind communities and persons to scriptural values.

The importance of narrative in communicating enduring truths and in transforming lives beyond the horizons of the original writers is abundantly evident. Every major world religion has a set of more or less consistent narratives at its heart, essential to the text (oral or written) that inscripturates its spiritual vision.[6] Whether by instinct or intent, narratives become essential seams in the fabric of any religion that will not be torn from its original design. Thus, history consistently indicates that those who wish to challenge the design of any religion begin with an assault on the canonical narratives.

ESTABLISHING COMMUNITY

Stories activate a sign system that allows the preacher and the listener to gain common perspective on an aspect of experience. When propositional truths are viewed through these narrative signs, understanding of biblical meanings and values are shared throughout a faith community. Without such signs for developing a consistent vision of truth, the community's values will not only shift, but its cohesive bond will be lost. Church-building and faith continuity require the sharing of narratives in which individuals share the sensations, emotions, decisions, and experiences of those who espouse or exemplify the community's truths.[7]

The loss of narrative spells the loss of community, because without narrative a church must endlessly frame new contexts in which to understand its propositions—forever changing their meanings as a result. Consistent or at least shared narratives do not preclude new applications of community values, but they do preclude a community without values. Stanley Hauerwas explains:

> What we require is not no story [sic], but a true story. Such a story is one that provides a pilgrimage with appropriate exercises and disciplines of self-examination. Christians believe scripture offers such a story. There we find many accounts of a struggle of God with his creation. The story of God does not offer a resolution to life's difficulties, but it offers us something better— an adventure and struggle, for we are possessors of the happy news that God has called people together to live faithful to the reality that he is the Lord of this world. All men have been promised that through the struggle of this people to live faithful to that promise God will reclaim the world for his kingdom. By learning their part in this story, Christians claim to have a narrative that can provide the basis for a self appropriate to the unresolved, and often tragic, conflicts of this existence. The unity of the self is not gained by attaining a universal point of view, but by living faithful to a narrative that does not betray the diversity of our existence.[8]

In order for values to be shared among individuals and communities that are diverse, separated by time, geography, and circumstance, those values must be shared through narratives that allow the principles to be relived through or re-experienced.

Propositions standing by themselves are inadequate intermediaries between transcendent values and particular peoples. Theologians and preachers must conscientiously strive to keep their statements in intimate contact with the narratives that endorse and explicate their convictions. Writes Michael Goldberg:

> Neither "the facts" nor our "experience" come to us in discrete and disconnected packets that simply await the appropriate moral principle to be applied. Rather they stand in need of some narrative that can bind the facts of our experience together into a

coherent pattern and it is thus in virtue of that narrative that our abstracted rules, principles, and notions gain their full intelligibility.[9]

Biblical truth comes alive, makes sense, and is communicated as its propositions are contextualized in the narratives that act as a transcendent "semiotic" (the technical lingo for a sign system), bridging cultures and individuals by enabling others to share the experiences that signal meaning.

ESTABLISHING TRUTH

The experiential sign system provided by the narratives of Scripture not only anchors biblical values for successive generations of believers, it also forms a bulwark for faith against the assaults of twentieth-century relativism. Typical of such assaults is that launched by Ernesto Grassi in his book *Rhetoric as Philosophy: The Humanist Tradition.* He writes, "Not only is every access to religious sacred texts closed to us but so also is the possibility of a metaphysics, a science that tells us about the 'essence of man.'" Grassi asserts that Scripture has no real meaning because it cannot be proven to have any definite meaning. This modern humanist concludes that access to divine truth is impossible as a result of two parallel lines of reasoning.

Truth Based on Spiritual Convictions

The first line is the most transparent and traditionally accepted. Grassi points out that because the object and origins of religion are not scientifically provable, sacred texts cannot logically reveal absolutes for everyone.[10] This observation is hardly novel and, in fact, contains a foundational assumption of most Protestant faiths (and modern Catholicism outside the Scholastic tradition). The central lines of Western Protestantism as represented in the Heidelberg Catechism, the Belgic Confession, the London and Philadelphia Confessions, and the

Westminster Confession, while valuing empirical evidences for the truths of the faith, nonetheless affirm that ultimate conclusions rely on spiritual convictions. The Westminster divines wrote:

> Yet notwithstanding [these evidences for biblical authority], our full persuasion and assurance of the infallible truth and divine authority thereof, is from the inward work of the Holy Spirit bearing witness by and with the Word in our hearts (Westminster Confession of Faith, 1.5).

Orthodox Christianity does not allow itself to be circumscribed by materialistic proofs. The words of religious discourse that Grassi relegates to irrationality are the truths already confessed in orthodoxy.

The Challenge of Subjectivity

Grassi's second line of reasoning is the less typical. He argues that even if faith concepts could be scientifically proven, they would remain relative. Grassi joins the chorus of philosophers of the twentieth century who have shown how modern science is blind to its own subjectivity. Even scientists can see only in the light of what they have seen. Their hypotheses are always dependent on current knowledge and contexts. Just as Newtonian physics had to give way to Einstein, and relativity to quantum theories, current scientific thought remains experientially based and is only as absolute as the current experiment or the expertise of the evaluator. Thus, even if religion were to meet the litmus test of empirical proof, faith would remain subjective. Ultimately, no two persons could share the exact same conditions for knowing and, therefore, the thought of each—though rational—would be limited to that individual. An empirical religion would remain subjective and incommunicable, according to twentieth-century reasoning.

The nature of Scripture's claims enables us to challenge Grassi's conclusions about the uncertainties of faith. Even if religious discourse is presuppositional and rationalism is subjective, human faith is inaccessible and incommunicable only if the presuppositions of the religion are false. Cornelius Van Til, one of the great defenders of faith in this scientific century, has demonstrated that presuppositionalism is not relativism nor subjectivism.[11] To operate within a circumscribed set of principles or normative standards that are coherent, logically consistent, and communicable, is not relativistic if the Spirit enlightens the mind, opens the heart, and directs the will. The "spectacles" of the Spirit, using the words of the Scriptures, are necessary if we are to know anything of God. This does not mean everyone understands the Scriptures, because the Spirit goes "wherever it pleases" (John 3:8). Yet this does not mean the church needs to apologize for subjectivism simply because the reality is not apparent to all. It is not subjectivism nor relativism for the sighted to flee a raging bull, simply because the blind do not see it. Fleeing without knowing the cause of the fright nor the path of safety would be relativistic, but since the work of the Holy Spirit opens spiritual eyes, this is not the condition of believers nor their faith. Christianity is not relativistic simply because it is nonempirical.

The Narrative Mirror

The interpreter is not without experiential guidance on the Spirit-led course to understanding Scripture. The historical events recorded in narrative passages reflect, disclose, and anchor meanings for the propositions of Christian truth that they accompany. Their lived-body features provide a consistent experiential context in which those propositions may be illustrated, understood, and shared. For example, according to the writer of the book of Hebrews, aspects of the Mosaic economy in the Old Testament are "a copy and a shadow of what is in heaven" (Heb. 8:5). The details of these emblems, along with their administration, were carefully articulated because they were so important to the message God related through them. "This is why Moses was warned when he was about to build the tabernacle: 'See to it that you make everything according to the pattern shown you on the mountain' " (8:5). The apostle Paul clarifies the reason for the careful monitoring of the Old Testament illustrations: "These are a shadow of the things that were to come; the reality, however, is found in Christ" (Col. 2:17).

In essence, the writers of Scripture are describing a double semiotic system that the Spirit has designed through their messages. The Old Testament symbols and narratives are signs that point to Christ. We understand statements about him (and from him) more fully because of the body of Old Testament illustrative material that prepared for a New Testament age understanding of him. At the same time, the New Testament narratives of Christ's redemptive work reflect back on the features of the Old Testament, more fully illuminating their meaning and purpose. The signs of each testament mirror the images of the other, with the message of each mirror further illumined and clarified by the images in its counterpart.

EXPLAINING SCRIPTURE

Christ is the ultimate image and message of the historical biblical community. He clarifies all antecedent and subsequent scriptural images; but he could not be seen, known, or comprehended without the surrounding images that define him, even as he clarifies them. The narrative of his life is comprehensible by virtue of the narratives that precede him and prepare for an understanding of him. Yet the antecedent narratives are simultaneously made more comprehensible by the narratives of Christ's life—the Gospels unveil the full meaning of the preceding accounts.

The ways in which propositional meaning is established and maintained through narrative can be demonstrated within the biblical record. For example, a key precept of Old Testament law and New Testament theology is the decalogal imperative, "You shall not make for yourself an idol in the form of anything. . . . You shall not bow down to them or worship them" (Ex. 20:4–5). The propositional meaning seems clear enough: God must be worshiped without rival from the works of human hands. However, the primitive covenant people surrounded by idolatrous cultures struggled incessantly to get the message. Thus, God repeated this proviso of the covenant code in additional prophetic statements, but he did not rely solely on propositional echoes. The establishment and interpretation of the commandment's meaning was bolstered by a series of narratives that granted experiential definition to its propositional content.[12] The narratives pointed out what the proposition forbidding idolatry meant. They allowed individuals to understand what the commandments meant by unfolding their propositional content in experiential terms. Simultaneously, the biblical narratives affirmed that cultural values were effectively transmitted when propositions were linked with narratives.[13]

Mirrors of Bronze

The symbol of the bronze snake raised up by Moses in the wilderness (Num. 21) is one of the noteworthy images of the Old Testament that demonstrates the "time-binding"[14] elements of a narrative sign system.[15] The people of Israel had sinned and were punished with a plague of poisonous snakes. God instructed Moses to fashion a bronze snake, place it on a pole, and tell the people that "anyone who is bitten can look at it and live." The story is not immediately applied to past worship prohibitions or future worship interests, but the implications of the historical account become crucial in developing a comprehensive biblical understanding of what it means to obey the command against idolatry.

How fine a craftsman Moses was in his desert workshop we do not know, but we may assume that his bronze snake was a reasonable representation of the snakes that were afflicting the tribes. Still, Moses' creation became far more than a symbol of a snake. As a signifier of propositional truth, it took on a meaning that is not exhausted by the thing it most readily resembled, i.e., the vipers. Acting as a map to a larger conceptual territory,[16] the bronze smake is a special sign that makes visible an implied covenant between the Lord and his people. Beyond representing the snakes on the ground, the bronze snake signifies this covenant: "If you look on this object of faith in God you will experience divine healing."[17] The bronze snake thus becomes a signifier two times over. At a low level of abstraction it symbolizes the afflicting snakes; at a higher order of abstraction it symbolizes the implied covenant.

In terms of covenant and community development it is vital to note that in the narrative the bronze snake as a signifier always pointed away from itself to the thing signified. The snake on the pole was not venomous; it represented what was. More critically, the bronze snake did not heal; it pointed to God's healing hand and remained appropriate for God's people only as long as it retained its distance as the signifier. When the gap closed—when the signifier was misperceived as the signified—idolatry occurred. When Israel no longer considered the bronze image to be the hand pointing but the actual hand healing, then the serpent became an aberration of faith and an abhorrence to God.

Fencing the Field

To demonstrate the necessary distance between divine signifier and the divine essence, the Holy Spirit offers another narrative using the same snake image. King Hezekiah "broke into pieces the bronze snake Moses had made, for up to that time the Israelites had been burning incense to it" (2 Kings 18:4). The use and abuse of the symbol in the historical accounts of Numbers and 2 Kings create fences to define the field of meaning for the prohibition against idolatry. A symbol that had an immediate reference assumed a larger meaning in the scope of the biblical record. Succeeding generations could determine if they met the propositional requirements of the law by recounting the stories that defined its standards. Seeing these narratives establish such standards by both positive demonstration and negative example expands our understanding of their use in establishing propositional truths.

The narratives in which the same bronze snake has contrasting positive and negative roles create a dialectic that acts as a clarifying tenet of the commandment against idolatry for all faith traditions holding the accounts dear. The narratives teach both Christian and Jewish communities that there must always be a distance between that which points to God and God himself. Whenever those things that symbolize his covenant are actually taken to contain or actuate the covenant, they become idols rather than tokens of grace and, thus, transgress the Sinaitic commandment. Only in aberrant forms do Jewish and Christian traditions allow signifiers (symbols representative of the covenant, such as the bronze smake) to become the signified (things containing covenantal power in themselves). The Judeo-Christian heritage in its orthodox forms never allows the object to become the essence or to confine God to a thing. Things only point to God; they are not God.

Redeeming the Image

Not only does the dialectical character of these narratives create a context for interpreting the commandment against idolatry that is accessible across time and cultures,[18] but the stories also provide a sign that prefigures and clarifies the central message of Christianity. In the New Testament, the bronze snake reappears. Jesus, in foretelling his crucifixion, explains the spiritual significance of his being lifted up on the cross by comparing it with Moses' lifting up of the bronze snake: "Just as Moses lifted up the snake in the desert, so the Son of Man must be lifted up, that everyone who believes in him may have eternal life" (John 3:14–15). Enriched by the accounts of the initial use and subsequent abuse of Moses' handiwork, Jesus' words "redeem" the symbol of the bronze snake. He once again uses the snake symbol as a sign pointing to the healing power of God's covenant, revealed in the Savior and appropriated by faith. The new symbol of the covenant (i.e., the lifting up of the Son of Man on the Cross) is explained, at least in part, by the narrative treatment of the older symbol. The meaning of the cross cannot be exhausted by references to the previous accounts, but much of the significance of Calvary can be understood because of its orientation to the previous signs that explain it, even as it distinguishes their meaning more precisely.

With the confirmation and clarification of earlier accounts, New Testament readers understand that the healing offered through Christ is based on the faith that those who look to him will live. By virtue of the same accounts New Testament believers understand that this faith is entirely the cause of their healing, since no work of human hands should be considered to have healing power in itself. The Old Testament narratives lend historic credence and experiential understanding to the New Testament proposition that the Cross alone is the key to life. The message of grace revealed in the Cross and more fully developed in the apostolic literature (e.g., Eph. 2:8–9) is safe-guarded and prefigured by the narratives that precede, circumscribe, and illumine it.

As the uses of the bronze snake accounts illustrate, the scriptural narratives can form a sign system whose culture-binding and value-transmitting abilities secure propositional truth. By tying propositional truth to narrative exposition, the Holy Spirit unshackles the Word from statements that could be culture-specific, time-bound, and individually twisted. With the testaments creating a system in which a first set of signs establishes orientations for the second set's interpretation, which itself further defines the import of the initial signs, the biblical writers create a belief system that is accessible across time and distance. The system remains tied to its presuppositions, but it is not mired in cultural vagaries that obscure the essence of faith. Backed by direct propositional statements and historical facts, the narratives of Scripture create biblical understanding that can be retrieved, repeated, and shared.[19] The narratives accompanying the propositions of Scripture ensure the communication of biblical values in ways the propositions alone could not.[20]

EXPOUNDING THE STORY

Not only do biblical narratives help us understand how to communicate meanings and values consistently, but their divine use also helps preachers understand how to communicate God's message if they are to preach biblically. We can duplicate the pattern provided in the Scriptures, which functions both as a precedent and a norm for our own expounding of biblical truth. Since Scripture's truths are imbedded in narrative, the reiteration of those truths—or at least the interpretation of them—should not be divorced from narrative exposition. Life-situation illustrations, far from disengaging an audience's focus on a passage, may refine listener understanding of the passage's meaning in the very manner Scripture itself employs.

Mimicking Scripture

In other words, life-situation illustrations mimic the narratives that facilitate meaning and value transmission through biblical accounts. As we noted earlier in this chapter, such illustrations possess the ability to cross time barriers and thus build community. This ability of life-situation narratives to create bridges of truth across vast human differences is vividly demonstrated by an illustration that is now nearing its second millennium of use. The following Talmudic narrative that has never gone out of vogue relates the message of the providential care of God in the face of apparent affliction. It is a story told of Rabbi Akiba after the destruction of the second temple:

> In the turbulent first century, the rabbi once traveled in a strange country where mystery still dwelt. He had taken with him three possessions—an ass, a rooster and a lamp—and had stopped at night in a village where he hoped to find lodging.

When the people there drove him out, he was forced to spend the night in a forest nearby. But Rabbi Akiba bore all pains with ease, being heard always to say, "All that God does is done well." So he found a tree under which to stop, lit his lamp, and prepared to study the Torah briefly before going to sleep. But a fierce wind blew out the flame, leaving him with no choice but to rest. Later that night wild animals came through and chased away his rooster. Still later, thieves passed by and took his ass. Yet in each case, Rabbi Akiba simply responded by saying, "All that God does is done well."

The next morning he returned to the village where he had stopped the night before, only to learn that enemy soldiers had come by in the night, killing everyone in their beds. Had he been permitted to stay there, he too would have died. He learned also that the raiding party had traveled through the same part of the forest where he had slept. If they had seen the light of his lamp, if the rooster had crowed, or if the ass had brayed, again he would have been killed. And how did Rabbi Akiba respond? He simply replied as he always did, "All that God does is done well."[21]

This story of Rabbi Akiba serves as an ancient apologetic dealing with one of Scripture's most difficult issues: How can God be good and yet allow evil to occur in his world or to his followers? The narrative is notable, however, not only because it deals so forthrightly with the ancient problem of theodicy, but because it continues to reemerge in contemporary contexts.

Charles Swindoll now uses an illustration with many parallel features in order to communicate the mystery and faithfulness of divine providence to modern Christians:

There was once a fellow who, with his dad, farmed a little piece of land. Several times a year they would load up the old ox-drawn cart with vegetables and go into the nearest city to sell their produce. Except for their name and the patch of ground, father and son had little in common. The old man believed in taking it easy. The boy was usually in a hurry . . . the go-getter type.

One morning, bright and early, they hitched up the ox to the loaded cart and started on the long journey. The son figured that if they walked faster, kept going all day and night, they'd make the market by early the next morning. So he kept prodding the ox with a stick, urging the beast to get a move on.

"Take it easy, son," said the old man. "You'll last longer."

"But if we get to market ahead of the others, we'll have a better chance of getting good prices," argued the son.

No reply. Dad just pulled his hat down over his eyes and fell asleep on the seat. Itchy and irritated, the young man kept goading the ox to walk faster. His stubborn pace refused to change.

Four hours and four miles down the road, they came to a little house. The father woke up, smiled, and said, "Here's your uncle's place. Let's stop in and say hello."

"But we've lost an hour already," complained the hotshot.

"Then a few more minutes won't matter. My brother and I live so close, yet we see each other so seldom," the father answered slowly.

The boy fidgeted and fumed while the two old men laughed and talked away almost an hour. On the move again, the man took his turn leading the ox. . . .

Twilight found them in what looked like a huge, colorful garden. The old man breathed in the aroma, listened to the bubbling brook, and pulled the ox to a halt. "Let's sleep here," he sighed.

"This is the last trip I'm taking with you," snapped his son. "You're more interested in watching sunsets and smelling flowers than in making money!"

"Why, that's the nicest thing you've said in a long time," smiled the dad. A couple of minutes later he was snoring—as his boy glared back at the stars. The night dragged slowly; the son was restless.

Before sunrise the young man hurriedly shook his father awake. They hitched up and went on. About a mile down the road they happened upon another farmer—a total stranger—trying to pull his cart out of a ditch.

"Let's give him a hand," whispered the old man.

"And lose more time?" the boy exploded.

"Relax, son . . . you might be in a ditch sometime yourself. We need to help others in need—don't forget that." The boy looked away in anger.

It was almost eight o'clock that morning by the time the other cart was back on the road. Suddenly, a great flash split the sky. What sounded like thunder followed. Beyond the hills, the sky grew dark.

"Looks like a big rain in the city," said the old man.

"If we had hurried, we'd be almost sold out by now," grumbled his son.

"Take it easy . . . you'll last longer. And you'll enjoy life so much more," counseled the kind old gentleman.

It was late afternoon by the time they got to the hill overlooking the city. They stopped and stared down at it for a long, long time. Neither of them said a word. Finally, the young man put his hand on his father's shoulder and said, "I see what you mean, Dad."

They turned their cart around and began to roll slowly away from what had once been the city of Hiroshima.[22]

The Talmudic allegory and the evangelical illustration could hardly be from more diverse sources: ancient Judaism and modern American evangelicalism. However, despite this cultural distance, the narratives communicate a consistent understanding.

Transcending the Gap

These stories—though varied in some detail—reflect a consistent "narrative pattern" that transcends cultural differences and communicates religious understanding. The time- and culture-binding features of narrative are especially evident in these parallel accounts in two remarkable ways. First, two widely differing religious communities that find much difficulty in communicating on other planes actually share some religious values through these narratives. Because the divergent constituencies can existentially reenter and reexperience the truths of the narrative, they can share an element of religious understanding in spite of obvious differences in their faith. Narratives demonstrate an amazing ability to transmit meaning and values to people separated by time, space, circumstance, and religious systems. If such narratives can transverse understanding chasms between faith communities, surely they can help span the gaps between pews, not to mention the abyss between pulpit and pew.

Transcending Logic

Perhaps an even more notable feature of the value of narratives illustrated by these two stories, however, is evidenced by the type of truth they communicate. We have demonstrated how life-situation illustrations clarify and support propositional truth. Theodicy, however—that paradox of religion which must prove that God accomplishes good with evil for which he is not responsible—creates propositional absurdity. To understand theodicy by relying on logic alone will never fully satisfy us. Narratives, however, are not dependent on mere logical reflection or syllogism. Values that the logical mind finds too difficult to prove become acceptable and accessible through the dynamics of experience.[23] Life-situation narratives communicate with the clarity of experiential affirmation what propositional statements can only begin to explain. What we affirm with "I know, I can see it, I've been there," carries far more personal significance than abstract logical reductions.

Life-situation illustrations that personally involve listeners create expository proof. We accept what we experience as being real, as having a truth foundation.[24] Even when we cannot logically or propositionally make sense of the totality of the message, we "understand" its truth if we live it. Thus, life-situation illustrations that incorporate the dynamics of experiential narratives may function as an effective means of biblical exposition where propositions alone might fail. Such illustrations may call for conclusions and create affirmations that neither cold logic nor bald statement could transmit.

Notes

1. Ian MacPherson, *The Art of Illustrating Sermons* (Nashville: Abingdon, 1964), p. 7. MacPherson actually failed to read some important works on the subject, but his argument is still valid. Note also, John Dowling complains as early as 1848 about the paucity of information relating to the craft of illustration in *The Power of Illustration* (Colby, 1848), p. 24, as quoted by Dawson Bryan (*The Art of Illustrating Sermons* [Nashville: Cokesbury, 1938], p. 11), who makes the same complaint a century later.
2. W. E. Sangster, *The Craft of Sermon Illustration* (London: Epworth, 1946), p. ix.
3. Bryan, *The Art of Illustrating Sermons*, p. 16.
4. Charles Haddon Spurgeon, *The Art of Illustration*, Third Series of *Lectures to My Students* (London: Marshall Brothers., 1922), p. 2.
5. John Killinger, *Fundamentals of Preaching* (Philadelphia: Fortress, 1985), p. 106.
6. Dennis Davis, "Notes for a Proseminar on Narrative Theory," Speech Communication Departmental Proseminar (Southern Illinois University at Carbondale, April 25, 1986), pp. 1–2.
7. Rolf von Eckartsberg, "The Eco-Psychology of Personal Culture Building: An Existential Hermeneutic Approach," *Duquesne Studies in Phenomenological Psychology*, ed. Amadeo Giorgi, Richard Knowles, David L. Smith III (Atlantic Highlands, N.J.: Humanitas Press/Duquesne University Press, 1979), p. 228.
8. Stanley Hauerwas, *A Community of Character: Toward a Constructive Christian Ethic* (Notre Dame: University of Notre Dame Press, 1981), p. 149.
9. Michael Goldberg, *Jews and Christians, Getting Our Stories Straight: The Exodus and the Passion-Resurrection* (Nashville: Abingdon, 1985), p. 242.
10. Ernesto Grassi, *Rhetoric as Philosophy: The Humanist Tradition* (University Park: Pennsylvania State University Press, 1980), pp. 103–4.
11. Cornelius Van Til, *A Christian Theory of Knowledge* (Nutley, N.J.: Presbyterian and Reformed, 1969).
12. Burke O. Long, ed., *Images of Man and God: Old Testament Short Stories in Literary Focus*, Bible and Literature Series, David M. Gunn, ed. (Sheffield: Almond, 1981), p. 7; Peter D. Miscall, *The Workings of Old Testament Narrative*, The Society of Biblical Literature Semeia Studies, Dan O. Via, Jr., ed. (Philadelphia: Fortress, 1983), p. 9.
13. Burke O. Long, *Images of Man and God*, p. 8; also see in *Images of Man and God*, James Crenshaw, "The Contest of Darius' Guards,"

    p. 88; David Gunn, "A Man Given Over to Trouble: The Story of King Saul," p. 111. Further insights on similar themes are offered by Michael Novak, "'Story' and Experience" and Stephen Crites, "Angels We Have Heard," in *Religion as Story*, ed. James B. Wiggins (New York: Harper and Row, 1975), pp. 54, 175–76.

14. Wendell Johnson, *People in Quandaries: The Semantics of Personal Adjustment* (New York: Harper and Row, 1946), p. 162.

15. The comments in this portion of this study result from reflection on an article by James VanOosting entitled "Moses, Hezekiah and Yale's Gang of Four" (*The Reformed Journal* [November 1983], pp. 7–8).

16. Johnson, *People in Quandaries*, pp. 131–32.

17. James VanOosting, "Moses, Hezekiah and Yale's Gang of Four," p. 7.

18. Anthony C. Thiselton describes this process in Godamer's terminology saying, "If a text is to be *understood* there must occur an engagement between two sets of horizons . . . namely those of the ancient text and those of the modern reader or hearer." See *The Two Horizons: New Testament and Philosophical Description with Special Reference to Heidegger, Bultmann, Godamer and Wittgenstein* (Grand Rapids: Eerdmans, 1980), p. 15.

19. Ibid., p. 16.

20. Stephen Crites, "Angels We Have Heard," pp. 26, 52.

21. Belden C. Lane, "Rabbinical Stories: A Primer on Theological Method," *The Christian Century*, 98 (1981), pp. 1308–9.

22. Charles Swindoll, *Come Before Winter and Share My Hope* (Portland: Multnomah Press, 1985), pp. 215–17.

23. Stanely Hauerwas, with Richard Bondi and David B. Burrell, *Truthfulness and Tragedy: Further Investigations in Christian Ethics* (Notre Dame: University of Notre Dame Press, 1977), pp. 25–30.

24. David Michael Levin, *The Body's Recollection of Being: Phenomenological Psychology and the Destruction of Nihilism* (London: Routledge and Kegan Paul, 1985), p. 64.

The Method:
Making Illustrations

Introduction to Part Two

Snapshots from Life

INSTRUCTIONS

An illustration is a snapshot from life. It captures a mood, a moment, or a memory in a narrative frame and displays that slice of life for the mind to see and the heart to know. If preachers are to take advantage of the narrative dynamics discussed above, they must develop illustrations that reflect the principles that make stories powerful instruments of communication. Phenomenology, the study of how the mind processes information, not only serves as a hermeneutical tool to explain how narratives work, but also acts as a guide to show how to construct illustrations.[1]

As we shift now from explaining to doing, we need good instructions. We must understand the phenomenologist's procedures if we are to use them to construct effective illustrations. Although the steps to be used can be analyzed separately to some extent, the actual processes are interdependent and synergistic.

Description

Description is our first task. Before we can understand an experience we must separate it from extraneous details and external presuppositions that interfere with our description of *this* experience.[2] Narratives that serve as illustrations of specific truths must be "bracketed" experiences, isolated from surrounding experiences. We slice events from life's continuum and free them from extraneous details that might communicate other principles. This procedure for constructing life-situation illustrations is the focus of the next chapter, "Framing the Picture."

Reduction

Reduction is the second step of phenomenological analysis. In this step we determine the essence of the experience we have bracketed. The process consists of "reflecting on the parts of the experience . . . and systematically imagining each part as present or absent in the experience." This procedure pares down an experience to its essentials so that extraneous details and secondary concerns do not complicate or cloud the analysis. A storyteller captures listeners (i.e., takes them into the story's confines) by eliminating distracting, inadequate, or misleading details that could divert them down other paths. How we do this narrative reduction is the subject of most of chapter 6, "Filling the Frame."

Interpretation

The final step of phenomenological study is *interpretation*. The preacher uses the results of the previous two stages to draw conclusions about the meaning of an experience. Interpretation sifts the information from description and reduction to discern what meaning or value the experience holds. If there is no interpretation, then there is no meaning. Preachers must somehow interpret the illustrations they use, for the raw data of an experience do not explain themselves. Thus, the section entitled "Focusing the Image" in chapter 6 will suggest ways to make sure listeners interpret the illustration as the preacher intends.

QUALIFICATIONS

We must consider two qualifications before applying these phenomenological principles to sermon illustrations. The first arises with a reminder that the goal of this book is to revitalize traditional sermon forms without substantially changing them; thus we avoid the hostility and inertia wrought by more revolutionary approaches (see chapter 1). By investigating what life-situation illustrations can do, and why, the intent has been to discover avenues within traditional preaching that can further today's preaching goals without abandoning yesterday's values. The aim has not been to suggest a radical overhaul of homiletics, nor to condemn newer forms, but to determine if there is a defensible rationale for reemploying illustrations with greater effectiveness and insight. This study encourages the use of a historic preaching tool whose tremendous potential to transmit meanings and values communication research now confirms.

This concern to bring to light the best that classical homiletical thought has to offer characterizes part 3 of this book. While the underlying theory being applied in these chapters borrows some phenomenological terms for the sake of clarifying communication principles, the author is well aware of the philosophical underpinnings—and spiritual limitations—of this "science."[3] As a result, the works cited are largely of homiletic origins. These sources indicate that the communication crisis in preaching may be greatly allayed by letting communication research reaffirm what many preachers have already intuited, that is, that life-situation illustrations work.

The second qualification derives from this attempt to unfold the principles of life-situation illustrations within traditional expectations. The following discussions are *not* intended to imply there is only one proper way to present illustrations. Phenomenology supplies a perspective by which to view these preaching components, but it in no way holds the final word on what Christian preaching should be. These guidelines are not meant to be normative for all illustrating. They are intended to suggest ways that illustrations can be used effectively in "expository preaching" in a manner consistent with sound research. Expository preaching, as one of the most classic of homiletical forms, does not require exhaustive definition here. Its primary goal is to explicate a text for a congregation. Sermons in this tradition use illustrations with the intent of making the meaning of the text apparent; thus, illustrations are not the focus of the sermon. In expository preaching, illustrations tend to be anecdotal, brief (relative to the body of the sermon), and told in order to illuminate specific propositions. These illustrative guidelines are offered with this classic preaching tradition in view.

Notes

1. Richard Lanigan demonstrates just such a procedure of converting a phenomenological hermeneutic to a practical method of explanation in an article presenting the roots and processes of phenomenology (see "The Phenomenology of Human Communication," *Philosophy Today* 23 [Spring 1979], p. 10). Amedeo Giorgi performs the same conversion in outlining a method for phenomenological research in "Sketch of a Psychological Phenomenological Method," in *Phenomenology and Psychological Research*, ed. Amedeo Giorgi (Pittsburgh: Duquesne University Press, 1985), pp. 8–22.
2. In the discussion of description, reduction, and interpretation, I am following the analysis of R. Lanigan, "The Phenomenology of Human Communication," pp. 6–8.
3. See the account of the author's own battles with phenomenology in *Standing Your Ground: A Call to Courage in an Age of Compromise* (Grand Rapids: Baker, 1989), pp. 47–49.

Chapter 5

Framing the Picture

Driving home near midnight from a church meeting that had lasted far too long, straining both energies and patience, I turned on the radio to relax. In the cocoon of my car, insulated by the night and soothed by the music of an easy-listening station, I felt the tension begin to drain out of me. Absentmindedly I hummed along with the tune as pop musician Dan Fogelberg sang the lyrics of a love ballad:

> Longer than there've been fishes in the ocean
> Higher than any bird ever flew;
> Longer than there've been stars up in the heaven;
> I've been in love with you. . . .[1]

Suddenly it hit me. Hey! I can use this song to explain God's eternal love in Ephesians 1:4–5 to my young people. The ballad is right out of their cultural experience, and if I isolate these familiar words and associate them with the less familiar biblical principle, they will be able to make the connection and understand.

ISOLATE AND ASSOCIATE

Just the snatch of a song was the catalyst for a process that is a first step in the craft of illustrating. You as the preacher isolate some event, conversation, perception, or relationship in your experience and associate it with the principle, concept, or proposition you wish to relate. In this way you provide a lived-body experience for your listeners through which they may contextualize and interpret your thought. The listeners need not randomly search through their own experiences to select events that explain what is being said—a process that is inefficient and beyond your management as the speaker. You must first isolate a life-situation experience with which the listeners can relate through parallel experiences of their own or through the vicarious experience provided by your description, and then associate that experience with the concept you wish to convey.

The process of isolation and association does not need to follow this order. You may see in the framing of the moment[2] an event or a sequence of events that reminds you of an associated concept (as the popular song reminded me of an element of God's love). Then you may file that isolated event away in your memory or in some catalog system until you are ready to make the association. But the reverse will work too. You may first formulate a concept or proposition and then venture on a safari through your own memory and perceptions in order to isolate and entrap an associated experience that enables you to show others what you mean. Such an expedition, with the resulting explanation, is exemplified in the following illustration:

> Some time ago I was struggling to find a way to explain a traditional understanding of the Atonement in a sermon I was preparing. The theological elements were apparent to me and conceptually already worked out in the sermon: God's requirement of holiness, the sin that precludes our ability to meet that requirement, and God's own loving sacrifice of his Son that provides humankind the means to meet God's requirement. The

problem was how to take these theological abstractions and make them real and accessible to the average person. No solution was immediately apparent to me.

Then one day a student whose wife had a doctor's appointment brought his four-year-old daughter to class. As the class was breaking up, the father, who was now juggling a stuffed teddy bear, miscellaneous puzzle pieces, a security blanket, and a half-eaten lollipop, along with his usual papers and books, took his knapsack full of heavy theology books and placed it on his daughter's back. "Help me carry some of these things will you, honey?" he asked. She smiled only for a moment and then feeling the weight of the burden she looked up to her father and cried, "Oh, Daddy, I can't. Please, help me." Immediately the father took this burden along with the rest he already had and put it on himself—and I had my illustration.

As this father required something of his child and yet took the burden on himself when she could not handle it, so our heavenly Father deals with each of us in the Atonement. The requirements we could not meet, the Father met for us by taking our burden of sin on himself through Christ's death on the cross.

Here the concept to be related was determined before an experience was isolated for an association with it. The process of isolation and association obviously, then, can fluctuate. But the two components remain consistent. The craft of sermon illustration begins when you as the preacher bracket an element of experience in order to give your listeners access to an associated concept, or an isolated experience may spawn the associated idea. Whatever the sequence of events, both elements operate together. If they do not, comprehension does not advance effectively. Louis Lehman reports what happens when an experience is isolated without association:

> I recently heard a well-known and very capable radio minister discussing Christ as the Bread of Life. He suddenly launched into a description of a visit he had made to a restaurant in New York, which specialized in all kinds of bread. It was interesting. I could smell the freshly baked loaves, steaming with goodness. I saw the thin bread sticks, savored the tangy cheese flavor in some, delightful onion in others. But I wondered what

was the point? To my amazement, there was no application made of this. He had a parable without interpretation.[3]

Without associations experience carries no pertinent meaning for the listener. Similarly, if an experience cannot be isolated from other experiences, it is questionable whether it carries any meaning. We cannot associate ideas with accounts that have neither beginning nor end, neither background nor development, nor have any identifiable details, placement, or sequence. Without characteristics to isolate them events are simply a blur in personal history.

The Sublime Ordinary

The preacher who wants to create illustrations must cultivate the ability to isolate and associate experiences. To do this, the common way of looking at the world, namely, as a passing parade of little consequence unless some clown comes by and tweaks your nose, must cease. Every passing form, color, and shadow holds illustrative promise. The preacher must look at the world marching past the eyes as a photographer looks through a camera, constantly framing one moment, one event, one sequence after another. What looks common to the ordinary eye is significant to the artist because of the peculiar shadow upon it, the colors in the background, or a tear upon a face that should be smiling. Preachers should be continually taking snapshots of both life's great and commonplace events so that they may relate both to the awe and to the tedium their listeners' experience. Nothing of life goes by without examination. If you hope to illustrate well, do not wait passively for the world to offer you something significant to note. Rather, steal from the world the treasures others do not notice or do not have the opportunity to display. There is beauty in a child's mud puddle, irony in a monument to a saint, pageantry in an abandoned city lot, and grief in a sagging barn, if the preacher will but see it.

The psalmist thought that the stars "poured forth speech"

about God (Ps. 19), and Agur saw God's providence in the home of a rock badger (Prov. 30:26). You too can see as much and show as much, if you are committed to relating experiential truths that people can feel and comprehend. This does not mean that you can, or should, look at every object or event asking, "Now, what does this illustrate?" Such concentration would rob you of movement through life and your enjoyment of it. Still, if you are a preacher, you can open your mind and vision to receive a spectrum of light and life that others do not usually see. You see in the ordinary that which discloses the sublime. Yours is a trained eye. Others see what you see; they do not see as you see. Edgar N. Jackson writes:

> The master of the art of seeing would keep his eyes on his Master, who used similar opportunities so effectively. He took the commonplace situations of life and filled them with a new meaning. He was able to dramatize problems in brief narratives so the people could see their problems walk before them. When they were able to see relationships objectively, they were able to think through their problems. They went on their way with new hope, new courage, and a new sense of purpose because they had found a new relationship with their God. Jesus, the master of insight, helped them to see themselves as they were.[4]

By showing others truths in terms of experience with their own world, not only do you enable them to comprehend theological principles, you enable them to see their world and lives in a new way.

The Illustrations of Life

Illustrations that isolate a life-situation experience and associate it with a conceptual truth re-create the medium through which listeners normally identify and comprehend meanings. D. W. Cleverly Ford writes:

> Admittedly, to quote from Dante, Dumas, Dostoievsky, and Dickens is impressive, but . . . what a congregation will most readily hear is references by the preacher to objects, events, and

people's comments which he has seen and heard himself *in the recent past in the locality*. An illustration drawn from the derelict house in the next street, the aftermath of a recent storm, a local flower show, a current play at the theatre, is the kind that is most serviceable.[5]

Not only do such illustrations reveal deep truths in readily accessible form; they also teach people to see their lives in the light of those truths. This is not to devalue the use of historical examples, fictional allusions, parables, fables, allegories, and other forms of illustration; but these other forms of illustrations are used most effectively if they desribe and relate to common experience in the form of familiar emotions, identifiable dilemmas, personal traits, or situational parallels with which listeners can immediately identify. Lehman writes:

> An illustration is a piece of life, a setting so familiar to the hearer, so totally believable, that a minimum of description enables him to see it and live it. Prod his memory or his consciousness, and he is in the picture, not just a spectator. If the illustration is well proportioned, well designed, well chosen, the hearer realizes that he has seen, heard, handled, felt, or experienced something identical to what the p/t [i.e., pastor/teacher] is describing.[6]

If a historical event is used for illustration, it too should be presented as a slice of life with enough description of setting, drama, and persons that today's listeners can yet find themselves in that event. If you must refer to the Spanish Armada, take care to capture the event. Isolate its human features. Let the listeners see the cannons flash, feel the storm waves, and fear the shoals—rather than have to tolerate another grade school lecture on the history of England and Spain, hoping it may "mean" something now, even though it never did before.

USE STORYTELLING TECHNIQUES: NARRATIVE EXPOSITION

Everyday experiences that are bracketed in terms of space, time, and/or relationships, as well as narratives of extraordinary events that elicit wonder, angst, or irony, can bring scriptural truth to life. There is no set formula for how such an account is related, but its very nature as a slice of time or portion of relationships implies it has a beginning and end, a background and some development, and some point to make. In short, it is a story. Many of the components of the story may be implied rather than stated, or assumed rather than articulated.[7] But illustrations that involve a listener's own experiencing of the truth are generally more than simple metaphor, allusion, or simile. Thus, when Dawson Bryan says, "Practically every illustration should be as technically perfect in form as a short story," he is not merely advocating good structure, but restoring a fundamental form of powerful communication.[8]

Since stories are crucial to effective communication, storytelling principles should serve as an organizing scheme for determining what illustrations should do and be. Bryan suggests four chief components of a good story: there is a beginning; there must be action; a climax is reached; the conclusion ends it.[9] Adam's list is essentially the same: background (briefly sketched), a complication or problem, suspense, climax, and conclusion.[10] These lists can be combined to create a model for effective illustrations. An illustration will usually have an introduction, descriptive details, movement (actual or emotional), crisis, and a conclusion. The remainder of this chapter shows how to set off and begin illustrations using narrative techniques. Chapter 6 explains how illustrations progress and conclude according to a story model.

INTRODUCING THE ILLUSTRATION

Illustrations used in preaching usually begin with an introduction. Just as sermons need introductions to arouse attention and broach a subject, illustrations need arresting beginnings, especially since they are often imbedded in expository passages or act as watersheds between main points. If the illustration is not properly introduced, its key features or intended impact may simply be missed.

All too often preachers begin an illustration with the tired and unimaginative "Let me illustrate . . . ," or a host of variations on this theme: "Here we have an even more striking illustration of such spiritual understanding . . . "; or, "Perhaps you will get this distinction best by a single illustration adapted from . . . "; or, "Here is a roadside experience taken from the paper which gives vividness to what I mean. . . ."[11] Deane Kemper rightly identifies this technique of illustrative introduction as lacking integration. Instead of involving the listener in the experience of the truth being related, such beginnings seem to put a wall between the illustration and the truth it is supposed to illustrate.

A dry, encyclopedic announcement that you are launching into a different sermonic mode makes the illustration seem formulaic or artificial rather than a part of the natural flow of your thought. It can also make the listeners feel patronized, as though you are slowing down to include them, or worse, throwing in an artificial hook to manipulate them. Of course, even these bearded techniques occasionally prove to be useful or necessary, but they should be used sparingly if you really intend to involve the audience in your thought. Kemper writes: "Examples and illustrations lose their power if introduced with 'a good illustration of this is . . .' which gives the impression that the preacher is trying to sell his or her own story. . . . Congregations can recognize illustrations without being told what they are."[12] Transition statements necessary to accommodate the eyes of a reader seem superfluous to a listener's ears if your entire manner indicates an illustration is coming.

Shifting Gears

In a real sense an illustration is an explanatory parenthesis coming before or after a passage of formal sermonic exposition. As such, illustrations are a change in the flow of things—not so much a break in the action as a shifting of gears. One of the simplest ways, unobtrusive yet effective, to introduce an illustration is simply to pause; to put in the clutch, as it were, in order to prepare for the gear shift.[13] This is particularly appropriate when the exposition has itself come to a summary that is pregnant with meaning and has listeners pacing the waiting rooms of their minds for an announcement of what the results of this delivery are.

For example, if you are preaching on the unholy pragmatics of King Saul in 1 Samuel 13, you might conclude the exposition with the summary: "People who think they will serve God in ways better than God himself has prescribed are only fooling themselves. You cannot do the will of God and break the Word of God." But what comes next? If you now digress into a lame "Let me illustrate . . . ," you cripple the power of the final phrase just turned. It is often better to let the thunder of "You cannot do the will of God and break the Word of God" echo in a poignant silence and then seize the power of that drama to drive home the point in real life. If you have just concluded your exposition with such a telling phrase, you might best serve that truth by letting your next words be as involving as these:

> A businessman in our community unexpectedly knocked at my front door several nights ago. The anguished look on his face told me immediately that something was very wrong. I invited him in. He sat on our sofa, and for the next two hours, often in tears, this respected businessman explained that his business largely depends on the production and sale of pornographic magazines. He told how over the years of seeing young women and children exploited he had agonized over whether to continue in his work. The look in the eyes of a child in one particular photo had seared into his heart and now haunted his conscience. But, said the man, he could not now leave his job. The security of his family and future required him to continue in this work in which he had established position, seniority, and a pension.
>
> What did he want from me? The man wanted me to assure him that, if he donated twenty percent of his income to the church, his occupation would be okay with God. In effect he was saying, "It is both in my best interest and in God's best interest that I keep this job; therefore, assure me that it is in accord with God's will."

I did not. Instead, I explained calmly, but as honestly as I knew how, what I have just told you, my friends: You cannot do the will of God and break the Word of God.

This man thrives on an industry that sucks the blood of human misery, and the infection of that filth threatens the eternal security of both himself and his family. For temporal pragmatics this man breaks the Word of God; the will of God is concerned for far more lasting consequences. Neither this man, nor any person here, can do the will of God and break the Word of God.

No artificial introduction should rob such a personal account of its drama and aptness. Stepping away from your own involvement in the message and distancing yourself from your audience by "putting them in their place" with a formulaic "let me illustrate," could well destroy the involving power of the illustration. Good illustrations are the direct result of your own reflection on the words you have spoken and the truths you have uncovered. Introducing that thought inartistically in encyclopedic expression and dusty archaisms inherently appears condescending, clumsy, or both. Lloyd Perry and John Strubhar write, "Do not talk about illustrating; just illustrate."[14] A pause will sufficiently introduce many an illustration. Combine the pause with (or substitute it with) a change of pace, or even a change of expression, and listeners will automatically know you have changed gears.[15]

Slicing Out the Context

What you are trying to accomplish with an illustration should determine the actual words that introduce it. If the modern communication researchers are correct, an illustration is more than a substitute explanation or subsequent clarification. As a re-created slice of life designed to involve the listener in what you are describing, you must isolate an illustration from other events and impressions.[16] You must move your listeners into another world—the "sliced-out" world of your illustration. The terms of your listeners' experience should mark the piece of life's cake you are now selecting for their nourishment. Introduce the illustration with familiar terms that set off the described experience in time, space, and/or situation.

Separation in Time

Jesus uses terms of time separation to introduce the parable of the workers in the vineyard: "The kingdom of heaven is like a landowner who went out early in the morning to hire men to work in his vineyard" (Matt. 20:1). Time features also contextualize the parable of the loaves at midnight in its introduction. Jesus says, "Suppose one of you has a friend, and he goes to him at midnight and says, 'Friend, lend me three loaves of bread'" (Luke 11:5). By identifying the time in which the events of the illustration occur the speaker frees the mind of the listener from the present time and allows flight to another world. We demonstrate this as parents when we intuitively begin the stories we tell our children with "Once upon a time. . . ." The principle never ceases operating. If you were to begin an illustration with "It was five minutes to midnight and she still wasn't home . . . ," you would move your audience to a dimension of experience separate from the pew in which they are sitting at 11:15 a.m. but, nonetheless, it is an experience to which they can relate and on which conceptual understanding can be built.

Donald Grey Barnhouse once used a time context to introduce an account of a personal conversation in which he explained how we get to heaven.

> Suppose someone came there [i.e., to your house] at three o'clock in the morning and put a ladder up to the second-floor window and began to climb in, what would you do? "Well," said the man, "I suppose I'd shoot him." I said, "What right have you to shoot a man? After all, can't a man come into your house in any way he wants to come?" He said, "No." Then I said, "You are saying that you can get into God's heaven any way, any time—by any back window that you choose. God Almighty has made definite, positive and absolute rules for entering His

heaven—rules as definite as our civilization makes—if you go to somebody's house you ring, you knock. As the Pennsylvania Dutch say, 'If the bell don't make—bump.' Make a noise and come up in the way that a house owner decides. . . . God has done the same thing. He says that anyone may come in, but they must come by the cross of Jesus Christ."[17]

The experience that explains the conceptual truth in this illustration is introduced by a time designation that is essential to framing the drama of the account.

Separation in Space

Terms of spatial separation may also introduce an illustration that needs experiential borders. Jesus begins the parable of the importunate widow by saying, "In a certain town there was a judge . . ." (Luke 18:2). The place of the illustration is more specific in the introduction of the parable of the Pharisee and the tax collector when Jesus says, "Two men went up to the temple to pray . . ." (v. 10). Again, it is important to remember these terms of spatial separation are more than simply a way of getting into the account. They begin the account by locating an experience so that it may be identified, grasped, and correlated. The mind's eye can visualize a place as well as a moment if you serve up an account sliced from the geography of our experience, as in this illustration underscoring the importance of every child of God:

> Rising out of the swamps just north of Savannah, Georgia, is a historic church named Jerusalem. Salzburg Lutherans built the church in the eighteenth century after being forced from their Catholic homeland. General Oglethorpe offered free land to those who would screen Savannah from hostile Indians, and the Salzburgers brought their faith to found the town of New Ebenezer. The name hearkened back to biblical images more solid than the bogs surrounding the town. The dangers of the land and the diseases of the swamps decimated the early settlers. But no trial could deter these stalwart Lutherans from their purposes. The few able-bodied men remaining climbed scaffolds to hoist

bricks up massive walls for their church. Women molded and baked sandy clay. Children carried the materials to each. To this day imbedded fingerprints of those children are visible on the brick exteriors. When you picture in your mind those little children transporting bricks their sick or dying parents could not carry, your heart can still break. But I imagine those children would rather your heart soar. For the print of each child is a poignant reminder that God can use even the little ones of this world for his enduring purposes. This church has stood for centuries testifying of God's faithfulness because of the efforts of children. No one is insignificant in God's Kingdom.

Separation of Situation

Separation of time and space can be combined in an illustration's introduction. Hence we get "A long, long time ago in a galaxy far, far away . . ." at the beginning of the *Star Wars* dramas. The combination reminds us that experience is not limited to only one or two dimensions and that an introduction to an illustration, therefore, may not as specifically indicate a separate time or space as a separate situation. The situation may be defined by the personalities involved (their relationships, accomplishments, or activities), by the event being recounted (its impact, import, or progress), or by your own reflection on your internal responses to an incident, account, or relationship. In the introduction to the parable of the sower Jesus simply says, "A farmer went out to sow his seed" (Matt. 13:3). No specific time or place is mentioned but, nonetheless, a particular situation is defined—a life experience with which the people could immediately identify. The same is true of many of the kingdom parables where Jesus says: "The kingdom of heaven is like a mustard seed, which a man took and planted in his field . . ." (v. 31); or, "The kingdom of heaven is like treasure hidden in a field . . ." (v. 44); or again, "The kingdom of heaven is like a merchant looking for fine pearls . . ." (v. 45); or, "Once again, the kingdom of heaven is like a net that was let down into the lake and caught all kinds of fish . . ." (v. 47). No precise time or place is specified in any of these introductory lines, yet each beacons a readily identifiable situation.

The great nineteenth-century preacher Charles Spurgeon quotes the Puritan Thomas Manton, who borrowed from classical history to combine elements of time, place, problem, and person to introduce a situation that drives home his premise:

> Cyrus, in Herodotus, going to fight against Scythia, coming to a broad river, and not being able to pass over it, cut and divided it into divers arms and sluices, and so made it passable for all his army. This is the devil's policy; he laboreth to divide the people of God, and separate us into divers sects and factions, that so he may easily overcome us.[18]

The situation is ancient and, in this writer's opinion, rather sparse on detail that would enable us fully to experience Cyrus's plight. But even with this economy of detail, the illustration works because it frames the event sufficiently to create an identifiable situation. Illustrations may much more effectively serve modern preachers if their introductions vividly identify the situations in which we find (or in our mind's eye could potentially find) ourselves.

Creating Involvement

Thomas Manton's illustration is purposefully quoted above, despite its limitations, because it touches on a type of illustrative introduction that should be approached with caution in the light of modern communication theory. By quoting from Herodotus, Manton automatically identifies the Greco-Persian Wars as the time-frame for his illustration. This time specification helps justify the use of what is otherwise a dubious way of beginning illustrations. Opening an illustration with a reference to a scholarly source may actually signal lack of pastoral wisdom. Too many illustrations begin with pastors simply displaying their library before the congregation. Dawson Bryan writes:

> It is wise to begin at once with the example. The introduction of author, title, and chapter usually has a deadening effect, and, because of such, many an otherwise good illustration is brought forth stillborn.[19]

This is more than a matter of artistic preference. By beginning with what the average listener could not, or has not, read, you as the preacher distance your listeners from your illustration rather than involving them. Further, if the literary work is highly specialized or theologically formidable, listeners may feel inferior (or infuriated) as a result of your display of "matchless knowledge." You are at less risk of alienating your audience if you involve them in the specifics of the illustration first and then relate the source as a matter of integrity later.

Martin Luther King, Jr., masterfully weaves together illustrative material and source credentials in his sermon "How Should a Christian View Communism?" He says:

> In America slavery could not have existed for almost two hundred and fifty years if the church had not sanctioned it, nor could segregation and discrimination exist today if the Christian Church were not a silent and often vocal partner. We must face the shameful fact that the church is the most segregated major institution in American Society, and the most segregated hour of the week is, as Professor Liston Pope has pointed out, eleven o'clock on Sunday morning. How often the church has been an echo rather than a voice, a taillight behind the Supreme Court and other secular agencies, rather than a headlight guiding men progressively and decisively to higher levels of understanding.[20]

The source of the material is practically buried in order not to distract the audience from the powerful images and allusions.

An alternative is simply to introduce the source in brief, general terms that communicate the sense of authorship rather than giving detailed and dull documentation. King displays such a technique in the sermon, "The Answer to a Perplexing

Question." Rather than spend time with unnecessary documentation of author, title, page, and source, King says:

> A modern humanist confidently affirmed: The future is not with the churches but with the laboratories, not with prophets but with scientists, not with piety but with efficiency. Man is at last becoming aware that he alone is responsible for the realization of the world of his dreams that he has within himself.[21]

The quotation illustrates a philosophical position King will attack by crystallizing the issues rather than clouding the mind with detailed source information. A sermon is not a term paper. Concepts can be lost in the oral recitation of documentation that is necessary for the classroom but has little purpose in the sanctuary.

The rule of thumb that extended source and author citations tend to make poor introductions to illustrations does not apply if you need the credentials of the source to make the illustration credible and to maintain audience involvement. In some cases the facts of an illustration are so debatable or so obviously beyond your expertise that you will lose listeners if you do not mention the source initially. In explaining our ultimate dependence on God's providence, Peter Marshall preached:

> I shall not soon forget the words of Dr. W. R. Whitney, a past president of the American Chemical Society, Fellow of the American Academy of Arts and Sciences, director of many vast electrical researches, as he made the simplest of all experiments.
>
> Dr. Whitney picked up from his desk a small bar magnet. He brought this near a steel needle, and the needle leaped to the magnet. Why? Dr. Whitney said: "We have worked out elaborate explanations. We speak learnedly of lines of force. We draw a diagram of the magnetic field. Yet we know that there are no lines there and the field is just a word to cover our ignorance. Our explanations are only educated guesses. . . .
>
> "So," explained Dr. Whitney, "after we are all finished with our theories and our guesses, we are still backed up against the fact of God—the will of God at work in what we call 'science.'"

> Thus, an eminent scientist looks beyond science (that some still think infallible and the source of all answers) for guidance.[22]

Brief source citations may also be appropriate for illustrative introductions if the source quoted is so well-known that the mere mention of author or title brings a gleam of recognition into the listeners' eyes, radiating "meaning" to them. Such sources include popular classics like *Huckleberry Finn, Robinson Crusoe,* and *Ben Hur,* widely accessible reading materials like this morning's Sunday school bulletin or yesterday's newspaper, appropriate movies, and even TV programs such as a classic "I Love Lucy" or a more contemporary situation comedy. Again, the key is audience involvement. Introductions that draw listeners into the experience of the illustration lead them to comprehend new meanings. Introductions that separate the audience from the experience deprive the illustration of its power to lead in any anticipated direction.

Snapping the Shutter

Those who take a snapshot of a vacation, a wedding, or a reunion take from that experience a slice of life that is meaningful to them. To take the picture, the photographer must trip the camera shutter. In doing so he or she separates this event or this moment from the surrounding experiences. Pushing the lever snaps the shutter that frames the experience. In a similar manner, when you as a preacher begin an illustration, you snap the shutter on a mental image that frames an experience in the minds of the listeners. If you do not press the shutter button distinctly, the picture will not take. Nothing will have been isolated from surrounding words and experiences. On the other hand, if you trip the shutter clumsily or set the wrong exposure, you will blur the picture. Extraneous details and overexposure to unnecessary elements damage the image being conveyed.

The narrative characteristics of illustrations offer many cues as to how they may be properly framed and kept from such damaging influences. The first step is to get the introduction right. The introduction sets off the experience being described from other experiences in the listeners' minds, framing it so that it can be viewed, appreciated, and understood. Of course, the illustration will still have no meaning if there is nothing inside the frame or if what is there is a mess. The task of the preacher—and the focus of the next chapter—is to determine what is necessary to fill the frame of an illustration with features that are clear and communicable. Again narrative research will be our tutor while scriptural precedent will be our teacher.

Notes

1. "Longer" (April Music, Inc., 1979).
2. Louis Paul Lehman, *Put a Door on It* (Grand Rapids: Kregel, 1975), p. 36.
3. Ibid., p. 89.
4. Edgar N. Jackson, *A Psychology for Preaching* (Great Neck, N.Y.: Channel, 1961), p. 74.
5. D. W. Cleverly Ford, *The Ministry of the Word* (Grand Rapids: Eerdmans, 1979), p. 204.
6. Lehman, *Put a Door on It*, p. 27.
7. Jay E. Adams, *Preaching with Purpose: A Comprehensive Textbook on Biblical Preaching* (Grand Rapids: Baker, 1982), pp. 90–91.
8. Dawson C. Bryan, *The Art of Illustrating Sermons* (Nashville: Cokesbury, 1938), p. 210.
9. Ibid., p. 220.
10. Adams, *Preaching with Purpose*, p. 93.
11. Bryan, *The Art of Illustrating Sermons*, p. 199.
12. Deane A. Kemper, *Effective Preaching* (Philadelphia: Westminster, 1985), p. 86.
13. Ibid.
14. Lloyd Perry and John R. Strubhar, *Evangelistic Preaching* (Chicago: Moody Press, 1979), p. 83.
15. Kemper, *Effective Preaching*, p. 86.
16. The terminology for "slicing out" life stories in order to communicate meaning varies greatly among the communication disciplines and philosophies, but the underlying methodology is consistent. Ralph Lewis says, "When the minister uses experience as proof . . . (1) he must clarify the experience; (2) he must intensify the

experience; and (3) he must make it real or interpret it" (*Speech for Persuasive Preaching* [Wilmore, Ky.: Lewis, 1968], p. 94); see also Jay Adams, *Preaching with Purpose*, p. 93. Richard Lanigan presents the classic phenomenological method for analyzing conscious experience through "bracketing," "reduction," and "interpretation" ("The Phenomenology of Human Communication," *Philosophy Today* 23 [Spring 1979], pp. 7–8). This methodology is specifically applied to communicating and interpreting life stories by Rolf von Eckartsberg (cf. "The Eco-Psychology of Personal Culture Building: An Existential Hermeneutic Approach," *Duquesne Studies in Phenomenological Psychology*, ed. Amadeo Giorgi, Richard Knowles, David L. Smith III [Atlantic Highlands, N.J.: Humanitas Press/Duquesne University Press, 1979], pp. 227–44).

17. Donald Grey Barnhouse, *Let Me Illustrate* (Westwood, N.J.: Revell, 1967), p. 228.

18. Charles H. Spurgeon, *Flowers from a Puritan's Garden* (Westwood, 1883; rpt. Harrisonburg, Va.: Sprinkle, 1976), p. 180.

19. Bryan, *The Art of Illustrating Sermons*, p. 199.

20. *20 Centuries of Great Preaching*, ed. Clyde E. Fant, Jr., and William M. Pinson, Jr. (Waco, Tex.: Word, 1971), vol. 12, p. 376.

21. Ibid., p. 365.

22. Ibid., pp. 37–38.

Chapter 6

Filling the Frame

INCLUDING CONCRETENESS AND DETAIL

Once an illustration has its introduction, the pastor must add details. But the associations the pastor intends to convey will mean nothing if the details are not focused. Ralph Lewis writes:

> Experience determines . . . [our listeners'] view of reality. They pragmatically judge every new idea they face by asking . . . , "Does it square with experience?" . . . If we are going to keep experience-centered listeners with us until the conclusion of our sermons, we must keep all parts of the message closely tied to experience.[1]

We need details that distinguish and identify. Things do not make sense to us if we cannot distinguish what they are. We know what we observe because we have handled, seen, examined, or felt some aspect of it.[2] We simply cannot interpret what does not clearly reach us through the intermediary of experience that operates in the world of specific sensations, perceptions, and feelings. Thus, for an illustration to communicate effectively through this medium, it must contain enough concrete details of the event being described to allow vicarious experiencing (or remembering) by the listener. "Other things being equal, the more specific and concrete an illustration is, the more powerful it is."[3]

Create the Reality

The reason concreteness empowers messages and furthers understanding is explained in simple terms by Webb Garrison:

> If I were to talk at length about my having been deeply moved by watching the setting of my son's broken arm, this would constitute a report of my feelings. But when I describe some factors that contributed to my mood, you are brought into the experience and feel with me. To re-create a moving situation is quite different from testifying to having been deeply moved.[4]

The more an illustration recreates the pertinent living details of the actual experience, the more it can communicate. As Fred Craddock says:

> The plain fact of the matter is that we are seeking to communicate with people whose experiences are concrete. Everyone lives inductively, not deductively. No farmer deals with the problem of calfhood, only with the calf. The woman in the kitchen is not occupied with the culinary arts in general but with a particular roast or cake. The wood craftsman is hardly able to discuss intelligently the topic of "chairness," but he is a master with a chair.[5]

The question is, "How?" How do preachers make an experience concrete and therefore applicable to their listeners? R. C. H. Lenski answers, "Concrete objects, persons, actions, situations, etc., are *fully described*" (italics added).[6] When Jesus tells the parable of the prodigal son, he does not relate the experience of the father's and son's reunion by saying, "The father expressed continued care for his wayward son." Jesus says:

> But while he [i.e., the son] was still a long way off, his father saw him and was filled with compassion for him; he ran to his son, threw his arms around him and kissed him.
>
> The son said to him, "Father, I have sinned against heaven and against you. I am no longer worthy to be called your son."
>
> But the father said to his servants, "Quick! Bring the best robe and put it on him. Put a ring on his finger and sandals on his feet. Bring the fattened calf and kill it. Let's have a feast and celebrate. For this son of mine was dead and is alive again; he was lost and is found." So they began to celebrate. (Luke 15:20–24)

The details that make the conceptual point are fleshed out fully to bring the illustrative experience to life. Christ describes perceptions, actions, dialogue, aphorisms, and changes of scene—all to express one illustrated concept: the father still loved his son. The details enable listeners mentally and emotionally to enter the situation they have not actually experienced.[7]

Lionel Fletcher once advised, "Don't hurry the telling of your illustrations. Tell them well. Build up the background, picture the whole scene, and make it live before the eyes of the congregation."[8] Nothing makes an account more real and alive to the listener than hard details in ample supply. When Billy Graham wanted to explain the importance of public commitment to Christ by comparing it to the commitment expressed in a wedding service, he did not say, "It's like getting married." He said this:

> Commitment involves the mind, the emotions and the will. . . . But I'm not really saved, I'm not going to heaven until my will makes the final decision.
>
> You know, when you get married you go before the minister. I had already fallen in love with my wife-to-be and I had asked her to marry me. She made me wait almost a year before she said yes, and it was the longest, roughest year I have ever spent in my life. Finally she said yes. The date was set, Friday, August 13, with a full moon, 1943. The minister stood there.

> I had already settled the fact that I loved her. I had already told her. I thought she was the perfect girl for me, but I was not married until the minister said, "Will you have this woman to be your lawfully wedded wife?" and I said, "I will," not that loudly but I said it. Now I wasn't married until I said, "I will." Then he pronounced us man and wife, publicly. . . .
>
> When you come to Jesus Christ in this crusade, you come publicly to say "I will" to Christ.[9]

The details make this illustration real and powerful. Not only are persons, dates, and scenes described, but emotions, dialogue, and even a bit of residual nervousness emerge in this most identifiable re-creation of a slice of life.

Truly excellent illustrations reflect this attention to detail to create identifiable experiences amid theological expressions. According to Lewis:

> Instead of starting with [or staying with] abstractions such as "mankind is mortal," we can begin with a concrete experience and say, "Deacon Adams died of cancer last month." We can give illustrations from the family- or work-life of our congregation. We can use common experiences such as birth, eating, walking, fishing to illustrate points or make analogies.[10]

Descriptive detail will make these illustrations live.

Bring It to Life

Human interest stories are not our only alternative. As Deane Kemper suggests, "Indeed, some of our most powerful sermonic images come from fairy tales, novels, and comic strips, to name but three sources of fiction. A story from either history or fiction will have greater interest and impact if told accurately, thoroughly, and with details in place."[11] Descriptive detail creates the analogy of common experience even when it is non-existent and explains why good fiction and popular histories are absorbing though they be fantastic and far removed from our everyday world.[12] Ancient events and fantastic accounts take on the dynamics of life-situation experience if we tell them with enough detail to involve the listener's memory, imagination, or vicarious experience. The key is providing enough information so that the listeners can "live through" the sensations of the experience that the preacher describes. In this way listeners relate the abstract concept of the sermon to what they have just experienced in the context of the sermon.

Stay on Track

Even though specifics are important, steer clear of details that are extraneous or extravagant. You should move the illustration to a point that clarifies or crystallizes a point of exposition. "Every word and description must point to the moral choice or dilemma. There must be no inadvertence or casual remark which would divert attention."[13] A student of mine once presented an illustration this way:

> After a career in the military, my father retired without clear plans for what he wanted to do. He aimlessly went from one entertainment and hobby to another, but nothing satisfied. He finally stumbled on a sculpturing course at the local junior college and found a knack he had always taken for granted was a skill few could match. He had a gift for making works of art which he had possessed all his life but never pursued. Now that pursuit has become his passion.
>
> When I went home this summer, I asked if I could help him. He quickly assigned me the task of using a rough comb to create the impression of fur on some clay bears he was making. I worked for hours and when I was done, I thought I had done a pretty fair job. But when I showed the bears to my father, he took them out of my hands and without a word began to refashion all that I had done. That hurt my feelings. It was as though all my work was unappreciated. I didn't appreciate that until I saw the results of my father's work. What I had done made the pieces look like clay bears with fur; what my father did looked like bears. When my father took over, he made things far better than I. In the same way when we turn matters over to our heavenly Father, he can manage them far better than we can.

This illustration has many fine elements, but extraneous detail clouds the first half. The listener is apt to think this is an illustration about the difficulties of retirement, the frustrations of purposelessness, or the discovery of gifts. The opening lines detailing the father's retirement woes introduce these subjects. But the illustration is supposed to be about our trust in the perfection of God's providence. The second half of the illustration gets to this point with pertinent details. Unfortunately, the first half diffuses the focus, diverts attention, and ultimately weakens the impact of the illustration.

Be Real

Descriptive detail is supposed to give an illustration the concreteness that makes it real enough to square with our experience. That intention will be thwarted, however, if the detail is not pertinent or not presented in common terms. Preachers may fall in love with the artistry of detail to the extent that they remove the illustration from any identifiable experience. "A certain amount of description becomes necessary to enable the listener to see the door and cross the threshold with you. This does not mean poetry—just description," says Louis Lehman.[14]

Of course, some preachers can present illustrations with wonderful artistry and beauty of language. Still, the chief goal is experiential identification, not the wowing of the audience with the speaker's gifts. In general, the trumpets and flowers may make the experience seem less real and limit the listeners' involvement in the experience being described. Unnecessary embellishments, inefficient story descriptions, and extraneous detail may so flood the listener's mind with irrelevant thoughts that no specific experience can be focused upon, lived through, and made meaningful.

Listeners need to understand as well as respect you as their pastor. You should describe difficult matters in decipherable terms even if more technical or erudite words would impress your listeners with your "amazing command of the language." For example, Bryan says that "much valuable assistance can be given to troubled souls by analyzing difficulties and conflicts. And yet such descriptions need to be given, not in the words of psychologist and psychiatrist, but in popular, understandable terms."[15] Spurgeon sums up the cautions in presenting illustrative description:

> We are not sent into the world to build a Crystal Palace in which to set out works of art and elegancies of fashion; but as wise master-builders we are to edify the spiritual house for the divine inhabiting [*sic*]. Our building is intended to last, and is meant for everyday use, and hence it must not be all crystal and colour. We miss our way altogether, as gospel ministers, if we aim at flash and finery. . . . Some men seem never to have enough of metaphors: each one of their sentences must be a flower. They compass sea and land to find a fresh piece of coloured glass for their windows, and they break down the walls of their discourses to let in superfluous ornaments. . . . They are grievously in error if they think that thus they manifest their own wisdom, or benefit their hearers. . . . The best light comes in through the clearest glass: too much paint keeps out the sun. . . . Our Lord's parables were as simple as tales for children, and as naturally beautiful as the lilies which sprang up in the valleys where he taught the people. . . . His parables were like himself and his surroundings; and were never strained, fantastic, pedantic, or artificial. Let us imitate him, for we shall never find a model more complete, or more suitable for the present age.[16]

While Spurgeon's ornamental discussion may in some ways violate the very principles he articulates, his point remains valid. Save the trumpets and flowers for occasions when eternity does not hang in the balance. How can people believe if they do not hear the Gospel, and how can they hear if they do not understand (cf. Rom. 10:14)? It is better to change hearts than turn heads. It is more important to make others wise unto salvation than to be thought wise.

Decipherable details can remove an audience from detached consideration of Scripture and actively involve them in a spiritual experience by creating the mental or emotional world in which truths can be seen and applied. Webb Garrison writes: "Words that name colors, shapes, sounds, odors, and other tangibles help create backgrounds that evoke moods. Anything that moves you can move your listeners—provided they are brought into firsthand encounter with stimuli that produced the emotion."[17] Preachers re-create the stimuli by presenting concrete, identifiable details in terms that are transparent enough to enable listeners personally to confront the tangibles that make the abstract real:

> As a child I spent summers at my grandparents' farm in Tennessee. A special part of that experience was getting up early and going down to the kitchen while my grandmother was making the morning batch of country biscuits. I loved grandmother's biscuits. I liked them so much that I would even sit at the kitchen table and sneak great globs of the sweet, gooey dough from the bowl and eat them like candy before she rolled out the biscuits.
>
> One morning as I chattered on about childish things— between smuggled bits of dough—my grandmother suddenly stopped me. "Stop! Listen!" she said. I stopped for a moment and, then, not hearing anything went back to my talking and chomping. But again she stopped me, "Stop! Listen!" This time she wiped her floury hands on her apron and walked outside to the porch. I followed her fearing the delay of my biscuits and gently chided, "Aw, Grandmother, it's nothing." "Stop, child! Listen!" she said with a certain urging that finally did make me stop. And, then, I heard it: the faint, desperate lowing of a calf in distress. "Quick, fetch your granddaddy," she said, and I ran through the pasture to get him.
>
> We discovered the calf in a distant barn entangled in cultivating equipment and bleeding profusely from a panic-induced struggle with the sharp tines. Even now our hearts go out to the helpless creature that would have died had I had my way and kept attention centered on what satisfied me. If only our hearts would go out to the creatures who are dying all around us without the Gospel because we are still concentrating only on what satisfies us. In our selfish pursuits we have grown deaf to the cries of their desperation. Perhaps you do not have every-

thing you desire just now and are questioning God. But before you blame God for his lack of compassion, examine first whether he is simply saying to you, "Stop! Listen!"

ADDING MOVEMENT

Illustrations must come to life. No one participates in an experience through a fixed stare. The world does not stand still to be observed. Where there is "meaning" there is action—even if it is only a mental scanning of the situation.[18] For the preacher this translates to the need of presenting illustrations in terms that communicate movement. Whether the movement is the transition of thought, the transfer of emotions, the metamorphosis of a relationship, or the motion of one's own body, the illustration must move to convey experiential meaning.[19]

In order to convey the necessity of forgiveness, among his followers Jesus told this vivid parable of an unmerciful servant:

> Therefore, the kingdom of heaven is like a king who wanted to settle accounts with his servants. As he began the settlement, a man who owed him ten thousand talents was brought to him. Since he was not able to pay, the master ordered that he and his wife and his children and all that he had be sold to repay the debt.
>
> The servant fell on his knees before him. "Be patient with me," he begged, "and I will pay back everything." The servant's master took pity on him, canceled the debt and let him go.
>
> But when that servant went out, he found one of his fellow servants who owed him a hundred denarii. He grabbed him and began to choke him. "Pay back what you owe me!" he demanded.
>
> His fellow servant fell to his knees and begged him, "Be patient with me, and I will pay you back."
>
> But he refused. Instead, he went off and had the man thrown in prison until he could pay the debt. When the other servants saw what had happened, they were greatly distressed and went and told their master everything that had happened.
>
> Then the master called the servant in. "You wicked servant," he said, "I cancelled all that debt of yours because you

> begged me to. Shouldn't you have had mercy on your fellow
> servant just as I had on you?" In anger his master turned him
> over to the jailers until he should pay back all he owed.
>
> This is how my heavenly Father will treat each of you unless
> you forgive your brother from your heart. (Matt. 18:23–35)

The power of the dramatic movements in this parable heightens
its impact. Individuals do not merely ask for mercy, they fall to
their knees and beg. The unmerciful servant does not merely
speak unkindly to his fellow worker; he grabs him by the neck
and begins to choke him. The account scans the subsequent
reaction and erupting emotional upset among the other serv-
ants, and vividly portrays the attitude transition of the master.
He moves from demanding payment with slave profit to
granting mercy, and then to commanding punitive imprison-
ment. The parable does not permit the removed observation of
static description. Listeners are gathered into the moment and
ushered through the experience by the descriptions of movement within the account.

Harry Ironside, long-time pastor of the Moody Church in
Chicago, captured key components of both physical and
emotional movement when he told of preparing a message
without sufficient audience analysis:

> I went to a mission in San Francisco years ago and sat for
> perhaps half-an-hour listening to marvelous testimonies of re-
> deeming grace. One after another rose and painted a dreadful
> picture of his past life and then told how God had saved him. I
> had come to that meeting with a little sermon all made up, but as
> I sat listening to these testimonies, I said, "O dear, my stupid
> little sermon! To think I imagined I could go into my study and
> develop a little discourse that would suit a congregation like this,
> when I had no idea of the kind of people I was going to address."
> So I just "canned" my sermon; I put it out of my mind, and when
> I rose to speak, I took this text: "And such were some of you: but
> ye are washed, but ye are sanctified, but ye are justified in the
> name of the Lord Jesus, and by the Spirit of our God." It was easy
> to preach to them then without a lot of study. These sermons that

you get up are so hard to preach, but those that come down are so much easier.[20]

Note first how Ironside introduces his illustration by framing it with a separation of place, time, and situation. Having isolated the experience, he at once moves his listeners into the event with action descriptions. No individual merely "tells" his salvation story, any more than Ironside simply "speaks." The former "painted a dreadful picture"; the latter simply "canned" his message. And both "rose" to speak. The references to physical movement do more than add coloring. Intuitively, Ironside involves the total person of his listeners in his experience. He tells of the growth of his own quiet panic and silent shame, because it is this mental movement (reflected in physical imagery) with which any preacher can identify who has suddenly seen something or someone unanticipated in an audience and has felt the cold wash of an unvoiced, "Uh-oh!" The world that we experience moves, and moves us. If preachers are to communicate by reflecting on the world outside or inside us, they must include descriptions of movement.

CREATING CRISIS

An illustration's movement carries the narrative forward to its crisis as the catalyst, or accelerant, of its fires. A good illustration must have a crisis. Not only is the crisis the conceptual hub of the experience that gives it significance and structure; it is also the experiential hook that translates listeners from the streams of awareness in which they live and transports them to the contexts of the message. "The daily life of the people in a congregation is a succession of crises. The story which would be of value to them in the heat of the day must rise into increasing tension until quite suddenly it reaches the breaking point, and then is settled."[21]

At the risk of sounding dialectical, the point of an illustration is in the *tension* its narrative details create. If you do not bring the audience to the edge of wonder, grief, anger, confusion, fear, or discovery, then your words have no point—no barb on which to hold meaning. The internal tension of an illustration holds the audience till some meaningful resolve because it spotlights the very types of experiences that bring members to hear your words and counsel.

In the parable of the Pharisee and the publican, the incongruous prayer attitudes of two men who are apparently moral opposites create the tension. The outwardly moral Pharisee prays "with himself" (Luke 18:11 rsv). The despised publican, however, "would not even look up to heaven, but beat his breast and said, 'God, have mercy on me, a sinner'" (v. 13 niv). The crisis for Christ's audience is determining what proper prayer is and deciding what it reflects about dependence on God's grace rather than self-righteousness. The complications in the details of the vignette create a tension between what these opposite men should be saying and what they are actually saying. Without this crisis the story holds no impact.

Narrative crisis does not have to be created by the threat of a tragedy. The complication may lie in a disclosure of facts or in a dissonance created by undisclosed facts. A crisis may be achieved by opening a door to scientific knowledge that was formerly closed or opening a new window from which to see the commonplace in a new light. At its heart, crisis is the tension of not yet knowing—not knowing the solution, not knowing the resolve, not knowing the punch line, or not even knowing how the punch line will be delivered this time. A crisis results from having sufficient, relevant facts to create a problem that the listeners have an interest in solving, forcing them to make the journey through the narrative in order to discover the treasure of resolution. The following illustration uses crisis to lead listeners on just such a journey:

> At a young people's meeting a fresh-out-of-seminary youth pastor attempted to impress his group with the wonder of the divine inspiration of Scripture. He gathered the teens in a circle, put a chair in the middle, and handed out Bible verses to

everyone in the circle. The idea was to blindfold someone sitting in the middle chair, have them tell the group some problem they were experiencing, and then have someone in the group read an applicable Bible verse as though God himself were answering through the words of Scripture.

The whole thing went miserably. The kids thought the whole idea was dumb. No one would talk about a problem more significant than how to get an A on Mrs. Bailey's math quizzes. Giggles rather than the voice of God predominated.

Then a new girl who had been sitting on the periphery volunteered to sit in the middle chair. The giggling subsided a bit as they blindfolded her because no one knew her well enough to know how she would take it. Then she spoke: "I don't know if I want to keep on with my life. I just can't stand it any more." Everything dropped to a dead silence. No one knew what to say or do and most just looked down in embarrassment or confusion. But one looking down saw the verse in his lap and read, "I am faithful; I will not let you be tempted beyond what you can bear. But when you are tempted, I will also provide a way out so that you can stand up under it."

"No one cares for me," said the girl. But then another girl in the circle read, "I have loved you with an everlasting love and drawn you with lovingkindness."

"You don't understand," said the girl in the blindfold with a voice now desperate; "my mother kicked me out today!" Someone said, "But Jesus says, 'I will never leave you nor forsake you.' "

That was all. They took the blindfold off the girl, and through her tears she asked, "Why doesn't God really talk to me just that way?" The youth pastor placed a Bible in her hands, put his arm around her shoulder, and tenderly said for her and for all, "The great thing about God's Word being inspired is knowing that he is talking to you just that way. God doesn't write in the clouds of the sky that blow away or speak in the night where only prophets can hear. He put his words right here in your hands where you can always read them and know that he is talking to you just that way."

Narratives usually introduce crisis elements early and resolve them late. In the case of the preceding illustration, a number of tensions probably arise early as questions in the listeners' minds: What is this youth pastor trying to do? Why isn't he succeeding, and why bring up something that seems to be failing? Who is this new girl? Is she okay? Will she be okay? What will help her? The crisis elements begin early and maintain a certain suspense that is only relieved by a conclusion that both releases tension and makes the illustrative point.

Crises heat the iron of thought that conclusions strike to form understanding. As the heat should be greatest just before the iron is struck, so the climax of the crisis is—under normal circumstances—placed as close to the conclusion as possible. As Bryan says, "The narrative must come to *a climax as near to the end as possible.* Everything is to build directly into the crisis and as soon as this climax is reached, or as nearly thereafter as possible, the matter must end."[22] The crisis sustains interest while pulling the listener even further into the experiencing of the situation. Having absorbed the listener as much as possible into the experience, the matter must now end and the point be made before interest, attention, and involvement diminish.

COMING TO A CONCLUSION

The illustration ends with a conclusion. Sometimes the climax of the crisis is the conclusion. The details prime the crisis, and the information necessary to resolve the tension suddenly bursts on the narrative landscape like an exploding artillery shell. In such cases it is wisest to leave the area without comment to demonstrate how powerful even the preacher considers the force of the matter. The listeners need no more words. They need only the emphasis of the explosion's echo in the silence of a concluding pause supplied by the preacher.

In driving home the importance of his words, Jesus concludes the Sermon on the Mount with just such an illustrative explosion. He compares those who build their lives on his words to a wise man who built his house on rock. Then Jesus concludes:

> But everyone who hears these words of mine and does not put
> them into practice is like a foolish man who built his house on
> sand. The rain came down, the streams rose, and the winds blew
> and beat against that house, and it fell with a great crash. (Matt.
> 7:26–27)

No other explanatory words are recorded. The point is made,
all questions are resolved, and the matter is left with that
cataclysmic crash to echo through the centuries.

In many illustrations, however, such conclusions may be
too abrupt. Listeners need more complete conclusions if they
are left questioning what the preacher meant by that story, or
whether the account is altogether over, or for what precise
purpose the illustration was offered. Usually a few words are
needed to supply the completion and resolution that relieve
and/or employ the tension of the narrative crisis. In a message
encouraging graduating ministry students to make the most of
their opportunities, David Calhoun offered one such illustrative
conclusion, using the biography of Charles Simeon, Cambridge
professor and missionary zealot in the nineteenth century:

> Simeon kept a portrait of the deceased missionary Henry
> Martyn over the mantle of his fireplace. Simeon had served as a
> spiritual father to Martyn at Cambridge, honing the young man's
> theology and inspiring him with missionary zeal. It was Simeon
> who saw Martyn off as he left Portsmouth and sailed for Asia.
> They never saw one another again. But for seven years
> Simeon constantly kept the novice missionary in his prayers
> through the young man's amazingly successful ministries in both
> India and Persia. Then came the terrible message. After only
> those few, fervent years word came to England that Martyn had
> contracted a disease and died on the mission field.
> A portrait of Henry Martyn, painted in India, was sent back
> to Simeon. He hung it in the honored place over his mantle so he
> could tell others the testimony of his young friend. Years later
> looking at the picture he would say to guests, "See that blessed
> man. No one looks at me as he does—he never takes his eyes off
> me; and seems always to be saying, 'The years are short. Be
> serious. Be in earnest. Don't trifle—don't trifle.' "[23]

The concluding words resolve and complete while driving home the point of this illustration. The growing tensions of the account could be framed in the questions: Why bring up so archaic an example? Why mention a dead protégé? What use was there in his dying? What purpose is served in the apparently unseemly display of the dead missionary's portrait? The conclusion completes the narrative by resolving these questions and thus finishes "bracketing"[24] the experience. The concluding details tie off the illustration as a complete conceptual and experiential unit.

The conclusion wraps up the illustrative experience. The introduction isolates the experience; the narrative exposition gives it form; the conclusion gives it definition. Without a conclusion the illustration never arrives; it unravels in delivery. A message is sent, but it trails away rather than leads to the point. Types of illustrative conclusions are too numerous to mention, but the essentials of effective ones are clear: (1) A conclusion indicates the completion of the unit of experience chosen for illustration by showing that the time, space, or situation is exhausted in which the experience occurs; and/or, (2) a conclusion indicates that the tensions, complexities, or problems internal to the illustration are resolved, or points out the reason they are unresolvable. Conclusions end illustrations by indicating the reason for stopping here—the picture is now finished; the event is now over; the thought is now complete.

FOCUSING THE IMAGE

What comes after the conclusion? This may seem an unlikely question since the conclusion would seem to end the illustration. It does finish the relating of the illustrative details, but it should not ordinarily be the end of the illustration dynamics. Much confusion exists in the homiletics texts over how preachers should make the transition from illustration to application. W. E. Sangster writes: "We have laid it down as a rule that an illustration cannot be a good illustration if it needs to have its point laboured. . . . Jesus never applied his par-

ables—and even then He did so only at the disciples' re-
quest."[25] But as conclusive as these words sound, Sangster is
soon forced to qualify his remarks: "This is not to say that a
man may not give the point of his illustration a couple of
hammer strokes when he has made it. Indeed he would be wise
to do so. But only a half-wit would confuse that with moralizing
and it should be done with clean, chiselled phrases which can
be driven swiftly and sharply in."[26] Curiously, Bryan makes the
same turn-around trip. After saying that "the good story does
not need comment," he retreats in the same paragraph to
"usually a few brief sentences are needed to relieve the tension
and bring the congregation back to the world around them, and
to enable them to feel the story a part of their own existence."[27]

Relate the Idea

The confusion lies in not making a proper distinction
between the exposition of the illustration and the relation of the
illustration. Life-situation illustrations act as a taxonomy by
which listeners use their own experiential world to understand
the truths the preacher wants to communicate. When as grade
schoolers we took a taxonomical chart into the woods and
discovered what type of trees were there by comparing their
leaves, bark, and shape to the chart, we were using someone
else's chart to discover certain truths through our own experience with them. Illustrations are the charts the preacher uses to
relate truths through the listeners' experiencing of them.
Occasionally the listener is already looking for a conceptual
pecan tree, and by using the preacher's illustration, knows he
or she has found it. Such an individual needs no further
instruction. However, more frequently preachers use illustrations in expository sermons to clarify, deepen, or apply an
understanding of propositions that seemed obscure, uninteresting, or irrelevant when first stated. In such sermons when
listeners are given a life-situation illustration, they are like a
child who has experientially discovered *this is a pecan tree*, but

still needs to be told its significance and how it can bring him fruit.

Events do not scan themselves. Preachers involve the listeners in the illustration through the description of an experience, but they must often still relate the specifics to the concept. Henry Davis adroitly observes:

> A human incident or a person contains many meanings, never just one, and the impression it makes on the hearer may not be that which the preacher intends. And, if to the hearer it suggests something other than the preacher intends, it competes with the preacher's thought, and does so with all the advantages of its innate power.[28]

Sangster demonstrates as much when he tells of another pastor's experience:

> A friend of mine, preaching with great clarity and skill on the text, "Ephraim is joined to idols," was startled, in being thanked afterwards to discover that he was being appreciated for the wrong thing. "That's what I say," said the enthusiastic worshipper. "Leave them with their idols. I never did believe in foreign missions myself."[29]

Distractions and differences always exist between preachers and their listeners.[30] Thus, having enabled listeners to discover experiential meaning through an illustration, the preacher still may need to state specifically how the details relate to the truths expounded. A few comments can easily illumine a truth in the brief glow of familiarity that life-situation illustrations create.

If Jesus did not apply certain illustrations, it was either because the point he made was so clearly stated near the conclusion that the relation was self-evident (as in the parable of the wise and foolish builders), or because the point was so dangerous to express that the truths of the parable were actually intended to veil meaning from those outside the inner circle. Mark records that when Christ was secluded, the Twelve and the others around him asked him about the parables. Jesus told them, "The secret of the kingdom of God has been given to you. But to those on the outside everything is said in parables so that, 'they may be ever seeing but never perceiving, and ever hearing but never understanding' " (Mark 4:10–12b). If one wants to argue from the parables that illustrations should be used without application in order to promote understanding, one must ignore Jesus' own reasoning for why the parables were used in public and why application was later made in private. As Mark goes on to explain in a key verse for this book, "He did not say anything to them without using a parable. But when he was alone with his own disciples, he explained everything" (4:34).

Once the narrative exposition of the illustration concludes, the preacher must still relate the details to the proposition being communicated. There are a number of ways that thought and illustration may play off one another, but usually the relation must be stated. Kemper writes:

> The example or quotation should be related directly to the point being made. It matters not at all whether the illustration precedes or follows the argument. The approach may be deductive with the point stated first and then illustrated, or inductive, with the illustration related first and the point made from it. Whichever approach is chosen, the relationship of principle and example needs to be made clear.[31]

Lehman chimes in with the observation that "the bridge from the illustration itself to the interpretation must not be shaky or ill defined."[32] The illustration needs to be related to the point being made. Usually this is done immediately after the expositional climax of the illustration while interest, involvement, and emotions are at their highest level.[33]

Apply the Truth

No mystery exists as to how to relate the illustration to the truth expressed—only a frequent neglect. The authors quoted in the preceding paragraph use a variety of terms to describe the "thing" that constructs the relational bridge from illustration to truth concept: the making of the point, the moral, the conclusion, the application, the interpretation. The variety of terms gives a healthy richness to our understanding of what the relational bridge should do, but it does not precisely identify what the structure is. Syntactically, the bridge is a "grouping statement" (or "interpreting statement"); that is, a sentence or two in which the preacher reaches into the illustration for details pertinent to the truth concept, extracts them, and then ties them together with the central idea being communicated.

Grouping statements demonstrate similarities between story details and propositional truths. The preacher might conclude an illustration with phrases such as "Even as so-and-so discovered this truth we must . . ."; or, "In the same manner . . ."; or, "We too must . . ."; or, "We learn from this account that just as. . . ." An alternative is to cap the illustration with an application phrased in wording parallel to a key phrase or thought that occurred within the illustration. An illustration might end with the statement, "Without his guide, Joe could never find his way back." The grouping statement might then be the parallel: "Without our God, we can never find our way back." Parallel phrases remove the need for prefatory comments indicating a relation is about to be identified, because such relationships are automatically implied.

Donald Grey Barnhouse made famous an analogy of the atonement, explaining that just as when a person looking through a green glass sees only green, and when looking through a red glass sees only red; similarly, when God looks at a sinful person through Jesus, he sees only his child. A variation of this analogy circulated in England many years earlier in an illustration that concludes with an expert grouping statement. Based on Isaiah 1:18 ("Though your sins be as scarlet I will make them white as snow"), the illustration went this way:

> During the late South African War I stood in one of our main thoroughfares watching a regiment of red-coated soldiers marching to the quay to embark for the front. A friend came up to me

and asked me what colour I thought their tunics were. "Why, red, to be sure," I replied. "Look through that," he said, handing me a bit of red glass. And to my amazement, when I looked through it, I saw a white-coated regiment pass before me! You look incredulous. It may seem improbable; but test it for yourself tomorrow. Get a piece of red cloth and view it through a red glass, and you will find the cloth becomes white. So with our sins. Though they are as scarlet, the red blood of Christ will make them white as snow.[34]

This is an excellent illustration from several perspectives. It takes a physical science principle, and through experiential description, adapts it to a relatable lived-body experience. Sense appeal, dialogue, and even some dialogical repartee with the listeners are included. But even with all these fine features, the author recognizes the need for a grouping statement that relates the pertinent features of the illustration to the point being made. The interpreting statement is short—two brief sentences—so as not to lose the momentum of the experience in driving home the main idea; but, still, the preacher takes the time to weld detail and thought together.

Good grouping statements can actually salvage botched illustrations. A preacher once compared the hardening effects of sin to an athlete's callouses in this way:

Many of you have played baseball. You know how at the beginning of the season when you begin swinging the bat in practice, you soon develop blisters and have to stop. But a good thing you can do is come back the next day and swing the bat a few times again. Then come back the next day and swing a few more times. Before you know it, by swinging the bat over and over, you will develop callouses and be able to hit home runs all day without hurting your hands. In the same way, when we repeat a type of sin day after day, we grow hardened to it. Our hearts callous over, and we sin without even feeling it anymore.

The main problem with the body of this illustration is that it seems to extol the very thing the preacher wants to condemn. Sin may act like callouses, but in the illustration the callouses are something *good*, enabling players to hit home runs. Yet despite this obvious flaw, the illustration seems to work. Why? Because the preacher reaches back into his illustration to extract only those details he needs when making his point. The grouping statement takes apparent confusion and organizes cohesive thought out of it.

Some very accomplished preachers occasionally dispense with such interpreting statements. However, this is usually possible only because what would be said in the grouping statement either has already been said in remarks preparing the listeners for the illustration or has been said within the narrative. Illustrations cannot function effectively without grouping statements at least being implied. The most eloquent of speakers explicitly make such statements most of the time with illustrations that truly are illustrations and not mere allusions. The grouping statement may not even be obvious to the speaker himself, and usually it does not appear in the magazine pages or anecdotal encyclopedias in which illustrations are published. This is because the grouping statements ordinarily come after the illustration's narrative conclusion. However, the speaker's unreported comments that usually follow the illustration almost always make a relation through some form of interpreting statement (as will become readily apparent to those who listen for such statements).

Illustrations, ultimately, are taxonomies by which experience discovers truth. No taxonomical chart ends with a blank. Somewhere there is a statement of what you have found— "This is a pecan tree." Without this statement that relates the experiential journey to some objective truth, features of the experience (while being interesting and absorbing) mean nothing—or, at least nothing confirmable. When you use a concise interpreting statement to tell your listeners what they have found with you, you are not abandoning your craft. Rather, you are serving your calling of making truth apparent.

Notes

1. Ralph L. Lewis with Gregg Lewis, *Inductive Preaching: Helping People Listen* (Westchester, Ill.: Crossway, 1983), p. 41.

2. Maurice Merleau-Ponty, *The Phenomenology of Perception*, trans. Colin Smith, rev. Forrest Williams (Atlantic Highlands, N.J.: Humanitas Press, 1981), p. 91.

3. Henry Grady Davis, *Design for Preaching* (Philadelphia: Fortress, 1958), p. 256.

4. Webb B. Garrison, *Creative Imagination in Preaching* (Nashville: Abingdon, 1960), p. 95.

5. Fred B. Craddock, *as one without authority* (Enid, Okla.: Phillips University Press, 1974), p. 60.

6. R. C. H. Lenski, *The Sermon: Its Homiletical Construction* (1927; rpt. Grand Rapids: Baker, 1968), p. 236.

7. Eugene Lowry, *How to Preach a Parable* (Nashville: Abingdon, 1989), p. 106.

8. Ian MacPherson, *The Art of Illustrating Sermons* (Nashville: Abingdon, 1964), p. 214.

9. *20 Centuries of Great Preaching*, ed. Clyde E. Fant, Jr., and William M. Pinson, Jr. (Waco, Tex.: Word, 1971), vol. 12, p. 311.

10. Lewis, *Inductive Preaching*, p. 41.

11. Deane A. Kemper, *Effective Preaching* (Philadelphia: Westminster, 1985), p. 87.

12. John Killinger, *Fundamentals of Preaching* (Philadelphia: Fortress, 1985), p. 30.

13. Dawson C. Bryan, *The Art of Illustrating Sermons* (Nashville: Cokesbury, 1938), p. 221.

14. Louis Paul Lehman, *Put a Door on It* (Grand Rapids: Kregel, 1975), p. 69.

15. Ibid., p. 203.

16. Charles Haddon Spurgeon, *The Art of Illustration*, Third Series of *Lectures to My Students* (London: Marshall Brothers, 1922), pp. 5–6, 11–12.

17. Garrison, *Creative Imagination in Preaching*, pp. 95–96.

18. Merleau-Ponty, *The Phenomenology of Perception*, p. 88.

19. Bryan, *The Art of Illustrating Sermons*, p. 200.

20. Faris D. Whitesell, *Power in Expository Preaching* (Westwood, N.J.: Revell, 1963), p. 78.

21. Bryan, *The Art of Illustrating Sermons*, p. 225.

22. Ibid., pp. 227–28.

23. David Calhoun, untitled address to graduating seniors of Covenant Theological Seminary, St. Louis (April 26, 1986).

24. See previous discussion on bracketing and "framing the picture" in chapter 5.

25. W. E. Sangster, *The Craft of Sermon Illustration* (London: Epworth, 1948), p. 88.

26. Ibid., p. 89.

27. Bryan, *The Art of Illustrating Sermons*, p. 226.
28. Davis, *Design for Preaching*, p. 256.
29. Sangster, *The Craft of Sermon Illustration*, p. 214.
30. Wendell Johnson, *People in Quandaries: The Semantics of Personal Adjustment* (New York: Harper and Row, 1946), p. 214.
31. Kemper, *Effective Preaching*, p. 86.
32. Lehman, *Put a Door on It*, p. 89.
33. Jay E. Adams, *Preaching with Purpose: A Comprehensive Textbook on Biblical Preaching* (Grand Rapids: Baker, 1982), p. 93.
34. *Cyclopedia of Religious Anecdotes*, compiled by James Gilchrist Lawson (Chicago: Revell, 1923), p. 16.

Part Three

The Practice:
Working with Illustrations

Chapter 7

The Character of Illustrations

Until now we have been demonstrating how life-situation illustrations form a critical part of the sermon by breathing life into the propositions that we as preachers hope to communicate to our congregations. But illustrations do more than simply help people gather information; they foster the relationship between pastor and parishioner by revealing us as their pastors, thereby rendering our preaching more effective. They also foster spiritual growth in our listeners as they learn to find themselves in the realities of Scripture.

TESTIMONY

Narratives reveal us. In our stories we explain ourselves to ourselves and to others. Julian Jaynes writes:

> We are always seeing our vicarial selves as the main figures in the stories of our lives. . . . Seated where I am, I am writing a book and this fact is imbedded more or less in the center of the story of my life, time being spatialized into a journey of my days and

years. New situations are selectively perceived as part of this ongoing story, perceptions that do not fit into it being unnoticed or at least unremembered. More important, situations are chosen which are congruent to this ongoing story, until the picture I have of myself in my life story determines how I am to act and choose in novel situations as they arise. . . .

But it is not just our own analog "I" that we are narratizing; it is everything else in consciousness. A stray fact is narratized to fit with some other stray fact. A child cries in the street and we narratize the event into a mental picture of a lost child and a parent searching for him.[1]

Mind Bonding

When you as a preacher isolate an experience in order to associate it with an idea, you clip a passage from the narrative of your life. You communicate by letting listeners enter the story of your own experience with the concepts you are trying to relate. Even if you do not detail how the experience affected you, your story exposes you nonetheless. Your reaction to the account—your experiencing of it—rises into view. Values, loves, and hates surface in your choices evident both in the story's creation and in how the story elements are associated with the concept being related. That account enables listeners to experience your own personal experience and, therefore, gain a parallel understanding of you.

For example, no one can immediately identify with the historical facts of Cortez burning his ships so that his troops would not be tempted to turn back from their exploration of the New World (though certainly the emotions of the men and the motivations of their leader could be made identifiable). But preachers who read that account may be touched by how, in a similar fashion, they wish they could destroy the temptations that lure believers to a past way of life. If you tell your parishioners the story of Cortez's actions, you not only re-create the event to relate the determination of Cortez and the angst of his men; by telling the account in the context of a sermon on temptation you also tell people the story of your own experience with that account. The story means something to you. By narrating it in the light of your experience, you inevitably share your experience with the listeners, thus enabling them to comprehend your thought. The narratives you select ultimately reveal your most personal perspectives— whether you intend them to or not.

Character Exposition

Behind every illustration lies your own personal story.[2] What causes you to think of the account? What makes you think it is appropriate? In what ways do you demonstrate your own depth of understanding and the reality or applicability of your message by the way in which your illustration uncovers and explicates the truth you want to espouse? In short, what do you tell us about yourself by the stories you tell? While the story explicitly told in a life-situation illustration aids scriptural exposition, the personal exposition implicit in such a narrative directly affects the reception of your propositions because it directly affects the listeners' reception of you as their preacher and pastor.

Any life-situation illustration (and, by corollary, the absence of any life-situation illustration) is a window not only to the meaning of the message but to the meaning of the messenger.[3] Your own personal story always shimmers in the background of any story you tell, witnessing to your own character, principles, and priorities.[4] We are our stories. They publicly evidence our psyches, our backgrounds, and our intentions by projecting the impact the Scripture we are expounding has already had on us.[5] In the telling of a life-situation illustration to explicate biblical truth we necessarily apply our thought to the realities of our world.[6] In doing so we inevitably reveal the world of our own reflection on that truth. In the illustration the preacher says, "This is what I think this means in my world." There is no room for retreat here behind theological abstractions and doctrinal prescriptions.[7] The truth is now out in real terms not only of what people should believe, but of who the preacher is.[8]

Ethos Power

The powerful way that the character or ethos of the preacher manifests itself in the telling of life-situation illustrations indicates yet another reason why such illustrations are essential for effective preaching. No premise has more consensus in classic and contemporary studies of rhetoric than the fact that the perceived character of the speaker is "the most potent of all the means to persuasion."[9] Roger Nebergall alleges there is no more consistent finding in communication research in recent decades than the discovery that the effects of message content alone in eliciting behavior change are minor in comparison with an audience's impression of a speaker's character and intentions.[10]

Because these powerful ethos dynamics are especially prominent in life-situation illustrations, such narratives are vital preaching tools.[11] Your personal trustworthiness as preacher has opportunity to shine through the telling of a story not only by the integrity and credibility evident in the specifics related, but also by the reasonableness or thoughtfulness of the application.[12] If your story indicates little regard for audience sensibilities, inappropriate idealisms, or unrealistic expectations, then the audience will feel they cannot trust your judgment.[13] Conversely, when these elements are well considered and managed, trust grows and potential effectiveness multiplies.[14]

If you never demonstrate that the noble principles you espouse have any connection with real life, your credibility will surely suffer. Many preachers shy away from illustrations they fear will make their preaching superficial, but without realizing that the complete absence of life-situation examples is more likely to make their preaching superfluous. If you cannot earth messages in the contexts that the congregation daily walks, then they will be forced to think you lack courage or insight for the real issues of life. Because a congregation's regard for your understanding, wisdom, and integrity has an opportunity to grow by applying religious precepts to the world in which they live, life-situation illustrations are particularly powerful when they demonstrate an expository truth as well as explain it.[15] Such "double-edged swords" not only elucidate a truth, they go on to show that the principle can actually work in real life and, thus, expand the likelihood that listeners will do what Scripture requires.

Apt Truth

You indicate a rich knowledge of your subject and your people when the truth you demonstrate is apt.[16] The latter is especially critical. By speaking to individuals in the contexts of their daily lives, you show you are genuinely interested in furthering their understanding rather than merely perpetuating your occupation. Instructors in past generations argued that preaching should contain only broad principles for the Holy Spirit to apply to individual hearts and situations. Such instruction perished with the recognition that generalization is the padding of sermons that allows most of us to escape Scripture's impact.[17] People need and want specifics. If even the one explaining the Bible seems unable to figure out how its truths apply somewhere in real life, then people fear the Gospel is a pipe-dream. But if you can demonstrate biblical principles with real-life particulars, then the truths have the ring of authenticity that makes your listeners more likely to apply them. Vicarious involvement provided by illustrations is the precedent individuals need to understand and respond to the Holy Spirit's instruction regarding their own situations.

People in your congregation automatically know by the illustrations you choose whether a sermon is practical and whether your knowledge, discernment, and intentions can be trusted. Illustration choices display your reasonableness and compassion—or your lack of these qualities. As Frederick Buechner says, it should not appear from the storm-tossed pew that you are the only one who does not see that the waves are twenty feet high. Meaningful life-situation illustrations prove you are concerned that people understand you and that you understand them. In this way illustrations demonstrate the primary element of ethos, i.e., good will.[18] Instead of being preoccupied with your own erudition or protecting yourself from possible contradiction in a cloud of doctrinal abstraction, you demonstrate a priority for audience understanding when you use life-situation illustrations.[19] And, to the extent that ideas presented challenge or correct, you even put yourself at risk in your listeners' behalf. When people see that you as pastor are willing to take such risks for their sake and the Gospel's, their appreciation of your character and compassion can add greater power to your message.

Of course, illustrations can contain any number of flaws that may immediately destroy the audience's belief in your integrity, judgment, and good will: old preacher's stories, improbable examples, pastoral counseling revelations, inappropriate family- or self-reference, name-dropping, and so on.[20] You should never forget that life-situation illustrations contain elements that spotlight your character and, as a result, powerfully affect the persuasiveness of the message. The story behind the life-situation illustrations—choices made in their selection, decisions governing their aptness, the choice even to use such illustrations—composes a weekly, personal testimony of how the Gospel has affected you.

WITNESS

Life-situation illustrations not only reveal the preacher, they also help people find themselves in the contexts of Scripture's realities. Though he does not use the term "life-situation illustrations," Killinger explains a remarkable function such illustrations provide in this fuller excerpt of thought cited earlier:

Personal illustrations. These are the ones, I confess, that I like best. Stories from men's and women's experiences, from children's experiences, narrated by the persons they happened to, shared by the preacher. There is a warmth about them that makes them very appealing. *They give an honest ring to the gospel that does not come from anything else.* They make the gospel seem real, touchable, truly incarnate. *They have the quality of witness, of personal presence that cannot come from another source.* [italics added][21]

By expressing truths through means that are accessible to others, preachers enable their listeners to see that their own experiences need not be unique.[22] The Gospel witness implicit in their illustrations serves to convince others that the truths cited can exist in their lives also. Witness urges others not to see themselves in isolation with their burdens and cares, but to see in another's story an answer to their problems. Witness seeks to present exceptional truth while inviting others to see and share its common application.

This element of witness in life-situation illustrations helps elevate sermons above the mere repetition of long-settled orthodoxy. When your story echoes in the story of the message in such a way that others can say, "That is the way I have felt," or, "I see how that would make sense in my life," the sermon has far greater potential actually to touch the vulnerabilities that lead to changed hearts. Allen intuits as much, saying, "There are no surefire methods which will insure that a given text will come to life. But I have found that whenever I am really experiencing a part of the biblical story as my story, the chances are greater that my hearers will experience it as theirs."[23] A sermon is more than the presentation of a homiletical product; it is the presentation of a person.[24] We preachers must share "not only the gospel of God but also our own selves" (1 Thess. 2:8 NRSV), because such witness opens the doors of the Gospel so wide that people can see themselves living in its contexts.

When individuals in the congregation sense that an element of biblical truth can "come to life" in the actual experience of another person, they begin to believe the truth may have some relevance to them. If your story demonstrates that you are a real person, in touch with real feelings and aware of real life, then you provide hope and encouragement to all who hear that the Bible speaks to today and for them.

HIDDEN TREASURE

The testimony of the preacher and the witness for the hearers that life-situation illustrations provide are frequently forgotten features of their persuasive value. The communication of scriptural truth is inseparably tied to your perceived character as preacher and the perceived reasonableness of what you attest. Sometimes preachers shy away from illustrations, fearing that they will rob the Word of its impact by surrounding it in fluff. How sweet it can be to realize that the illustrations congregations appreciate so much are such powerful tools for communicating scriptural truth and revealing your full understanding of the Word.

Like a backyard treasure overlooked because its wealth is hidden in the all-too-familiar, the value of life-situation illustrations can be hidden in the commonness of their use and content. You are most likely to see their real worth when you remember that those who learn to love and trust you through the truths you realistically apply are the ones most likely to receive the truths and do what you say.

Notes

1. Julian Jaynes, *The Origin of Consciousness in the Breakdown of the Bicameral Mind* (Boston: Houghton Mifflin, 1976), pp. 63–64.
2. This is an extension of Chaim Perelman's argument that as "the speaker provides a context for the speech, conversely the speech determines the opinion one will form of the person" (see *The New Rhetoric*, trans. John Wilkinson and Purcell Weaver [Notre Dame: University of Notre Dame Press, 1969], p. 319).
3. Ronald J. Allen and Thomas J. Herin, "Moving from The Story to Our Story," in *Preaching the Story* , ed. Edmund A. Steimle, Morris J. Niedenthal, and Charles L. Rice (Philadelphia: Fortress, 1980), p. 153.

4. *The Rhetoric of Aristotle*, trans. Lane Cooper (Englewood Cliffs, N.J.: Prentice-Hall, 1932), p. 230.
5. John Killinger, *Fundamentals of Preaching* (Philadelphia: Fortress, 1985) p. 115.
6. Norman Neaves, "Preaching in Pastoral Perspective," in *Preaching the Story*, p. 108.
7. Ibid., p. 108.
8. John F. Wilson and Carroll C. Arnold, *Public Speaking as a Liberal Art*, 4th ed. (Boston: Allyn and Bacon, 1978), p. 149; cf. Deane Kemper, *Effective Preaching* (Philadelphia: Westminster, 1985), p. 87.
9. *The Rhetoric of Aristotle*, trans. Lane Cooper, p. 9.
10. *The Rhetoric of Western Thought*, 3d ed., ed. James Golden et al. (Dubuque, Ia.: Kendall/Hunt, 1983), p. 294.
11. Ibid., p. 295.
12. Ian MacPherson, *The Art of Illustrating Sermons* (Nashville: Abingdon, 1964), p. 166; Thomas V. Liske, *Effective Preaching* (New York: McMillan, 1960), p. 200; W. E. Sangster, *The Craft of Sermon Illustration* (London: Epworth, 1948), pp. 90–91.
13. J. Daniel Baumann, *An Introduction to Contemporary Preaching* (Grand Rapids: Baker, 1972), p. 180; Liske, *Effective Preaching*, pp. 188–89.
14. Baumann, *An Introduction to Contemporary Preaching*, p. 250.
15. Louis Paul Lehman, *Put a Door on It* (Grand Rapids: Kregel, 1975), p. 73.
16. Liske, *Effective Preaching*, p. 199.
17. Edmund A. Steimle, Morris J. Niedenthal, and Charles Rice, eds., *Preaching the Story* (Philadelphia: Fortress , 1980), p. 108.
18. Killinger, *Fundamentals of Preaching*, p. 30.
19. Clyde E. Fant, *Preaching for Today* (New York: Harper and Row, 1975), pp. 8, 176–79.
20. Deane A. Kemper, *Effective Preaching*, pp. 88–89.
21. Killinger, *Fundamentals of Preaching*, p. 118.
22. Joseph Ruggles Wilson, "In What Sense are Preachers to Preach Themselves?" *Southern Presbyterian Review* 25 (July, 1874), p. 359.
23. Allen and Herin, "Moving from The Story to Our Story," p. 153.
24. Ibid., p. 161.

Chapter 8

Cautions for Effective Illustrations

When illustrations portray realism, integrity, and compassion, the persuasive power of a sermon trebles. Unfortunately, these characteristics are not automatic. Illustrations that are not carefully crafted may inadvertently undermine the pastor's character or erode a congregation's trust. Following are cautions to keep illustrations contributing to the preacher's efforts without creating barriers the message cannot penetrate.

DO NOT THINK MORE HIGHLY OF ILLUSTRATIONS THAN YOU OUGHT TO THINK

Illustrations are a means, not an end. The goal of a sermon is to present scriptural truth not to present illustrations. As helpful as illustrations can be, a sermon built on illustrations rather than on solid biblical exposition displays a dangerous shift of focus. Though the line may be thin between using a good illustration to build a sermon and building a sermon for an illustration, the distinction is real. The ministry of one who does not recognize the difference can easily be warped in ways not immediately recognizable. The preacher who constructs sermons to serve illustration rather than exposition inevitably drifts from pulpit to stage, from pastor to showman.

Focus

Any trained public speaker can select a theme and gather together a bundle of stories that will emotionally touch an audience—but this is not preaching. Snappy speech starters, canned anecdotes, and emotional climaxes do not make a sermon even if they capture and delight an audience. Only the Holy Spirit working by and with the Word of God in the hearts of men and women can effect the spiritual changes that are the mark of true preaching.[1] If explanation of the truths of the Bible does not have the highest priority in the pulpit, then no amount of combing through illustration files and preaching magazines can supply the material necessary to form a message worthy of the preacher's ultimate task. One can easily be deceived into believing that a sermon constructed primarily to please an audience has been wonderfully effective if its stories stimulate continuous waves of laughter or tears, but the deception is apparent if the truths of the Word are at all minimized, or even sacrificed, for the sake of popular reception. The proper focus of illustrations lies in presenting biblical truth in such a manner that it can be heard and applied, not in satisfying worldly perceptions of success.

Balance

Well-placed illustrations can give a sermon a sense of proportion and symmetry. Often the weight of traditional exposition needs to be counterbalanced with the relief and accessibility that good illustrations offer in order for a congregation to carry the whole load of the message. At the same time messages overloaded with illustrations damage the credibility of the preacher as hearers conclude, "All this one does is tell stories." Edward Marquart aptly labels such sermons "sky-scrapers," i.e., a construction of story on top of story.[2] Twenty minutes of illustration with two minutes of traditional exposition signals a sermon out of kilter. And twenty minutes of argument to two minutes of illustration is just as lopsided for most congregations.

Balance is not best achieved by a steel standard for the number and placement of illustrations, but by a common sense evaluation of how and where they will best make their point. Traditionally there is an illustration for each major division of a sermon.[3] Whether an illustration should come at the conclusion of all the subpoints summing up the main point, or immediately after a subpoint whose explanation is particularly difficult, or even as a transition showing the relationship between two points,[4] is better left to the discretion of the preacher who has the best feel for what the message as a whole needs. For instance, if a powerful illustration drives the conclusion of a sermon, it may be wise to use the illustration of the final main point early so that it does not impinge upon the conclusion's climax. If the illustration of the final main point and the illustration of the conclusion get stacked too closely together, the sermon's rhythm is thrown off and the impact of both illustrations is diminished.

Mass communication studies indicate that it is often best to use an illustration immediately after the first statement of an expositional principle in a main point's development.[5] The technique intrigues while introducing a subject and thus allows the point to be made with a minimum of attention drop or listener argument. This method is understandably popular with broadcast preachers.

Illustrations may properly appear at the beginning, middle, and end of a main point, as well as in the transition between main points. Such a conclusion underscores the seductive nature of illustrations. Once a preacher discovers how powerfully good illustrations elicit audience response and, then, further realizes they can surface almost anywhere in a sermon, the temptation is almost irresistible to use illustrations everywhere. We must resist the temptation. If we were to graph the emotional intensity of a sermon, we would see that the peaks tend to rise around illustrations, especially if an application comes with the illustration. But if a sermon is entirely illustrative climaxes, no portion holds exceptional impact. Preachers that load illustration upon illustration to woo an audience find themselves in a classic hedonistic dilemma. People lose interest in the commonness of the pleasure. Pastors also lose credibility in the shallowness of the thought that does not possess adequate expositional balance.[6]

If you were to list what a person most likely remembers from any well-prepared sermon, the list would look something like this:

Sermon Component Retention Hierarchy
Concluding Illustration
Introductory Illustration
Other Illustrations
Specific Applications (particularly if the listener strongly agrees or strongly disagrees)
Basic Idea of the Message
An Interesting Thought Expressed in the Message
A Main Point Statement
An Expositional Concept

The impression such a list leaves is that priority ought to be given to illustration rather than to propositional exposition, since people are not likely to remember the latter anyway. Such imbalance can easily occur when preachers begin to sense that illustrations are what congregations seem most to appreciate in their sermons. The imbalance will correct itself, however, when preachers remember that the list is incomplete. People remember the character of the one who presents the Word of God more than any sermon component. They hear a message, but they remember the messenger. If the impression they have of the preacher is that his sermons are entertaining but without depth of insight, then the credibility of the messenger is too badly damaged for the message to accomplish its highest purposes.

No matter where logical argumentation falls on a retention chart, it cannot be slighted without diminishing the impact of the entire message. Illustrations are best used when they further exposition, not when they are a substitute for exposition. For this reason the key terms of the exposition (particularly the subpoint terminology) ought to echo consistently in the narrative of the illustration, so that the priority on exposition stays in focus and the truth being expounded stays in view.

The nature of the sermon, the nature of the illustrations, and the nature of the target audience all bear on the proper balance of illustration in a sermon. Popular today in some circles is the narrative sermon which presents a biblical truth in a parable pattern. An extended story ending in a poignant moral or insight constitutes the sermon. We should not condemn this method since it was often Jesus' manner of teaching. Such sermons can serve important purposes, and the proportion of illustrative content in them is necessarily large. Still, a balanced perspective will recall that Jesus used such an approach in a context where he could assume his listeners knew (or would become acquainted with) much more biblical teaching. It is unlikely that Jesus believed a congregation would be fed adequately if its only diet were allegory.

One way to increase the illustrative content of sermons without damaging the message is by varying the types of illustrative material. As stated previously, full illustrations have sufficient lived-body detail to lead the listener into an experiencing of the truth being expressed. This means illustrations are narratives that will take some time to express, and explains why conventional wisdom advises only one for each major division of the message. However, this rule of thumb does not apply to abbreviated illustrative forms such as word pictures, vivid imagery, examples, quotations, and brief allusions. In fact, sermons are usually much more palatable if an illustrative philosophy and a variety of illustrative forms are liberally sprinkled throughout tough exposition, tenderizing the whole without reducing the meat.

Perhaps no variable should more determine the proper balance of illustrations in a traditional sermon than the nature of the audience. We can hardly expect a group of high schoolers on a retreat to appreciate tightly reasoned argumentation prepared for a group of professors. Audience demographics, the congregational situation, and pastoral purpose all should target a message and help govern the appropriate amount of illustration.

Preachers preparing messages for a congregation with a broad spectrum of ages, professions, and church backgrounds should normally plan to have illustrations in each major division of a message, including the introduction and conclusion. But application of this dictum should be highly variable, given the varieties of audiences and expectations that preachers face. The Westminster divines taught that sermons should be prepared according to the "necessities and capacities of the hearers."[7] This wisdom cautions preachers not to let their own preferences run roughshod over congregations' needs. A century ago R. F. Horton expressed this advice to pastors:

> Abstract modes of thought grow upon us [preachers] too easily when we spend much time in books and in the reverie of study. Illustrations become tiresome and impertinent to a trained thinker. The fascination of close and connected reasoning and of convincing the understanding by logical methods becomes ever more irresistible to a growing mind. To breathe in the higher circles of thought and to see the small matters of the field or market-place from a serene altitude is undoubtedly proper to a philosopher; . . . [but if a preacher only] studies diligently and exercises himself in the company of great thinkers, he is apt to become a philosopher and insensibly to drift away from common life and lose touch with ordinary people.[8]

While a preacher's preparation for ministry is necessarily academic, the preacher loses touch with what ministry is all about by mimicking the scholarly expressions of study manuals or trying to sound professorial enough to awe peers.[9] At some

point in ministry a preacher must decide: "Will I preach for
preachers, or will I preach for people?" The way you balance
the use of illustrations may well answer which path you chose.

Leverage

Determine when and where to use illustrations by assess-
ing what will make the message's application most effective.
The aim of preaching is not merely to explain what a text means
but to exhort God's people to do or believe what the text
requires. Explanation without purpose is senseless. So we best
use illustrations where they provide the most powerful leverage
for moving people to apply God's Word to their lives. In some
cases this will mean that illustrations must focus on clarifying
the exposition in order to allow sufficient understanding to
apply the text. In other instances it is better to use illustrations
to create deep feeling about a matter that is so familiar that it no
longer stimulates the response it should. Whether the leverage
we provide is intellectual, emotional, or some combination of
the two, illustrations work best when the preacher uses them to
affect the will of the hearers. Such use ennobles illustrations by
taking them from the realm of entertainment and placing them
in a servant relationship to a sermon's expository purposes.
Life-situation illustrations provide leverage for application
by establishing the fact that the truth advocated can be lived.[10]
Principles that have real world reference are not idealistic
mirages dreamed up by out-of-touch mystics. Life-situation
illustrations have the potential not only to make the truth
apparent, but to make the application seem attainable—a small
but vital first step in creating a willingness to do what Scripture
requires. People are simply more willing to attempt, or even to
consider, what they believe is possible. When they see spiritual
truth in scenes, incidents, and circumstances that form the
common ground of human experience, acceptance of what the
preacher says naturally grows.[11] Illustrations can carry compelling evidential weight.

When a sermon's application is controversial, illustrations

can prove particularly helpful. Though the argumentation of a sermon may be challenging, the images in an illustration can show the good will of the preacher.[12] Simple willingness to use an illustration may demonstrate to a congregation that the pastor is concerned enough about them to say things in a way they can understand. Still, in controversial messages the most persuasive feature of illustrations may be their ability to disarm or, at least, delay hostility. When a story starts, debate does not.

A story has the ability to lead hearers along a narrative trail into implications rather than immediately confronting listeners with arguments that raise their defenses.[13] At the same time that reaction is being delayed, real-life corroboration for what the preacher is advocating can be advanced in the details of the narrative.[14] Through illustration a skilled preacher can arouse attention, establish rapport, show care, state implications, quote experts, demonstrate realism, create sympathy or antipathy for individuals, sympathize with objectors, and disarm objections before leading to conclusions that might otherwise never be heard. The idea of such an approach is not to manipulate or soft-peddle the Word, but to keep ears open long enough to hear all God's truth.

Another reason people frequently give for not listening to sermons is that preachers address insignificant issues. A preacher may drone on week after week about matters whose lack of importance seems clearly conveyed by the fact that no one, often including the one speaking, seems to be very deeply moved by what is said. Logic dictates that if a matter does not seem very important, it probably is not. Here again illustrations can serve application through one of the very characteristics for which they are often criticized.[15] Illustrations stir the emotions. Because life-situation illustrations can deeply move people, they authenticate the importance of what is being said and give logical credence to the importance of the truth when it is applied to life.[16] Of course, emotional appeals can be artificial, excessive, and manipulative, but when they reflect genuine feeling they greatly aid a message's persuasion.[17] Sermonic application served by appeals to both the mind and the heart best reflects Scripture's own intent and approach.

DO NOT THINK LESS HIGHLY OF ILLUSTRATIONS THAN YOU OUGHT TO THINK

Though illustration serves exposition and application, its powerful effects on these primary features of a sermon challenge preachers to use illustrations conscientiously, carefully, and well. An illustration may force a sermon far off course or even destroy its impact if not handled properly. Illustrations are not such slight matters that they can be prepared with less care than any other sermon component. This is true because illustrations not only expound the text but also expound the pastor. Pity the preacher who does not realize that illustrations draw pastoral integrity, sensitivity, and sensibility to the foreground of the message. We need to avoid several cliffs along the path to illustration if our character and the sermon's message are not to become casualties of pastoral negligence.

Ill-prepared

Lack of preparation often mars illustrations. Despite years of observing and teaching preachers, I have never been able to grasp why so many of us assume that brilliant illustrations will magically materialize in our messages. We will write exhaustive outlines of our exposition, list five precisely phrased applications, but circle one word on a page for illustration. If I ask for a fully written sermon manuscript in a class, I always anticipate at least one student asking, "We don't have to write out the illustrations, do we?"

The assumption made in training and often carried into practice is that the great thoughts of a message are in the exposition. Illustrations are considered so incidental that whether one prepares them carefully or not is expected to have no real affect on the message. But careless preparation of illustrations can do incalculable damage not only to the surface presentation of a message but to the deeper potential it could have possessed had each aspect been prepared with the respect owed a vehicle for God's Word.

Some do not want to work hard at illustrations (or other sermon features) because they think such labor indicates their gifts are not great. They assume that if they had real gifts and more experience, illustrations would come easier. Such preachers may put themselves under the "discipline" of little preparation to advance themselves to the ranks of those who are so good "on their feet."

Apocryphal stories of Spurgeon to the contrary, good preachers are good because of hard work. Ministers who cease working hard live off their reputations rather than continuing to advance in excellence. Louis Paul Lehman writes, "The reality is you must see the figure clearly, and you must have a precise plan for making others see it. The only torment worse than having others wonder what you were trying to say, is to be uncertain yourself as to what you were trying to say."[18] If the details are to lead precisely to the point you are making; if the manner of delivery is to support content nuance and drive the climax home; if fumbling for phrasing and struggling for plot development is to be avoided; if the wording is to be appropriate for the target audience; if the interpreting statement is to mine the contents accurately and present the concept powerfully; then, you need to prepare well. As further cautions will indicate, there is no good substitute for hard work in crafting powerful illustrations.

Untrue

While lack of preparation signals lack of conscientiousness and inevitably damages the perceived character of the preacher, no greater damage will be done to people's estimation of their pastor than if they discover he does not tell the truth. Unfortunately, if a lie appears in a sermon, it usually comes in an illustration. Soon after a preacher discovers the power of illustrating, the additional impact of being able to say, "This happened to me," or "I thought this up," becomes highly tempting. The beacon of self-attestation is so powerful that preachers are often drawn to its flame when they have no business being in its vicinity.

If it is not true, do not say it is. One of the most common reasons that preachers neglect this simple dictum is that they recognize a tale is more powerful the closer it seems. Thus, even though the incident happened to someone else, they relate it as though the experience is their own. W. E. Sangster cautions against such fibbing with the "I" with apt illustrative flair:

> The assumption, I suppose, which lies behind this deception, is that the point would lack pith unless it were told in the first person. But a man who does this often soon forfeits the respect of his hearers and occasionally exposes himself to a public humiliation as well. A few years ago, at a religious conference, a well-known preacher evoked a storm of laughter by telling a good story as illustrative of his point. The story was received even better than he expected. As the laughter rolled towards the platform, in wave after wave, his expression seemed to say: "Well, I knew that that was a good story, but I didn't think it was as good as that."
>
> He was sublimely unaware that the same story had been told earlier in the evening by a speaker who had addressed the meeting before he, himself, had arrived, and who was sitting near him on the platform sharing his embarrassment at the prolonged mirth. Mr. A had told it of Mr. A.; Mr. B. had told it of Mr. B. The conclusion to which some of their questioners came afterwards was that it had not happened to either of them. It is not possible to remain entirely at ease when you find an audience laughing at you and not at your story. People do not laugh aloud in church when a preacher errs in this way but something dies in them. . . .[19]

As a preaching instructor I hear three to five sermons a day. This helps me get a good idea of what illustrations (new or old) are currently making the rounds in America's pulpits. I especially love discovering illustrations I can use. But sadly I often hear these same illustrations presented in the first person by preachers I respect. Too often preachers think that illustrations provide them some sort of "poetic license" with the truth. Unfortunately, their reputations and ministries will suffer for the lying which they allow themselves but which no congregation will tolerate when it is discovered.

Closely akin to presenting an illustration in the first person when the facts are not so is claiming credit for an illustration not one's own. A preacher who did not invent an illustration should not present it as though he did. Again, damage will be done to a pastor's reputation if he presents an illustration as his own one week and the congregation hears it from another at the community Thanksgiving service the next week. Preachers should recognize that there is no necessary harm in using an illustration from the communal repertoire that builds up in preaching circles over the years, but it is likely people will hear the story again or have heard it before.[20] All suspicions of self-promotion or plagiarism are immediately allayed if the preacher introduces an illustration (or includes somewhere in the telling) a phrase such as, "The story is told that . . . "; or, "I've hear it said . . . .'; or, "Once it was reported that. . . ." Such phrases do not muddy up an illustration with unnecessary bibliographic citation but protect the preacher from giving a false impression. Simply make sure you give the credit away if it is not rightly yours to take. Even if these little phrases are hardly noticed by the congregation, they can provide the preacher's own heart with a sense of integrity that will add confidence and authority to the message. No task in the world is more difficult than calling others to holiness with a tainted conscience.

The taint on integrity is most dangerous when the tale itself is untrue. No pulpit sophistry should allow a preacher to invent matters that suit the sermon and present the fabrications as truth. It is not wrong to come up with fictional accounts that drive home a point (so long as the message overall does not begin to pick up a fictional cast). One simply should not present a fiction as truth. You need not belabor the fact that the account is fictional but make sure everyone understands what is true.[21]

Again, there are important phrases to learn that can be said in half a breath that protect a pastor from suspicion or attack.[22] To begin an illustration with "What if . . . "; or, "Let us suppose . . . "; or, "I can picture it this way . . . " alerts all that what immediately follows is not true even though it illustrates truth. What follows such a phrase can be very near to life or highly fictive. In either case, the reputation of the preacher is protected and the point still made. Preface in a similar fashion accounts that have an origin in truth but need to be "dressed up" or "embroidered" in order to serve a point. It is better simply to acknowledge the "improvements" or present the account as fictional than to present a matter one's friends or family know did not happen quite that way.

In summary, the reputation of the pastor and purposes of the Gospel are best served by observing a few simple rules: (1) If it is not true, don't say that it is. (2) If it is not yours, don't imply that it is. (3) If it is not accurate, don't pretend that it is.

Inaccurate

Illustrative inaccuracies may be inadvertent rather than deliberate, but such lapses of fact also damage speaker credibility. Preachers often make themselves appear very foolish trying to sound like experts about matters outside their normal study or expertise. The "example from science" is particularly susceptible to challenge from the engineers, educators, and true scientists in the congregation.[23] Frederick Farley describes a preacher in another generation who ignored such advice to his own regret:

> In the early days of the motor-car [he] tried to illustrate conversion by pointing out that it was better to turn a car around and face in the opposite direction if it was found that a wrong direction had been taken, than to drive the car very far backwards. The illustration might have served very well if he had not used language which betrayed his ignorance. He spoke of "reversing the engine," and a motor-engineer pointed out to him

> afterwards that an engine is never reversed. It continues to operate in the same way, only it is connected with a gear which drives the car in the reverse direction.[24]

In this day of advanced technologies preachers need to research their examples carefully. Everyone makes mistakes, and even the experts differ on some explanations of facts, but Einstein did not invent the light bulb, X-rays do not light up the bones, modern submarines are not powered by gasoline, and Mount Saint Helens did not erupt due to cold fusion. Be sure you understand the scientific example before you try to illustrate with it.

Adept handling of facts instills listener confidence in a preacher. Congregational confidence soars when names, dates, and places are accurately cited. Impatience settles in rather swiftly, however, with references to "the Christian commitment of Benjamin Franklin," "the ninety-three theses of Martin Luther," "Churchill's famous line, 'We have nothing to fear but fear itself,'" "the prison ministry of John Colson," "the Hallelujah Chorus of Franz Joseph Haydn," and other equally appalling gaffes of preachers who have not bothered to get their facts straight. Accurate details in an illustration help establish the preacher as an authority, add credibility to the rest of the illustration, and help win a hearing for the message as a whole.[25] Inaccuracies undo all the same. The simple moral is, if you don't know for sure, look it up. Get the facts straight.

Improbable

An account may be true but still damage a preacher's credibility if it is so improbable that it strains credulity. I have occasionally tried to tell how the sun broke from the clouds on a rainy day to send a shaft of light down on our new church at the precise moment and at the precise point that the new steeple was being raised. Then as soon as the work was done "the divine imprimatur" departed. I have sequenced pictures of this event. I have witnesses by the score. I even have videotape. But if ever I try to tell the account just as it happened, I invariably get raised eyebrows, questioning glances, and snide comments at the door after the sermon. Since I cannot show a videotape with the illustration, I now choose not to use it. Rather than clarifying my point, I have discovered that this illustration's improbability makes people doubt me. Instead of fighting for the right to use an incredible-but-true illustration it is best to remember the couplet of John Gay:

> Lest men suspect your tale untrue,
> Keep probability in view.

Unrealistic

Closely related to the illustration that is improbable is the illustration that is unrealistic. The former makes a congregation suspect the reality of the event, the latter makes a congregation doubt the realism of the preacher. The best illustrations have a strong identification factor. Listeners believe they can know or do what a preacher is explaining because they see the truth in a world familiar to them. Jesus' own preaching should make it clear that illustrations that touch the most hearts rarely come from references to "perfect" saints or superspirituality. Illustrations from the lofty clouds of spiritual idealism ultimately destroy listeners' willingness even to hear what a preacher has to say. J. Daniel Baumann explains why with the eloquence of pastoral experience that is difficult to improve upon:

> Illustrations must be real. Many are guilty of idealism which frustrates the serious Christian. We talk about living the life of faith and who do we discuss? A man like George Mueller, who brought thousands and thousands of dollars into the orphanage in Bristol through simple faith, is established—though quite inadvertently—as a norm for Christians to follow. We talk about prayer by relating the experiences of a man like Praying Hyde, who spend twenty-four consecutive hours on his knees. The difference between Praying Hyde and ourselves is unbearable. When we talked about the "committed Christian" we remind the listeners of Hudson Taylor or C. T. Studd. What happens? These

great ideals, so removed from our life experience, produce frustration and despair.[26]

Of course, we are to use the lives and examples of extraordinary men and women of faith to inspire others in their Christian walk today. But to present such examples as normal or readily mimicked cheapens the significance of these saints' walk and denies most ordinary men and women the hope of ever taking similar paths. Were the events and the examples not extraordinary, we would have no record of them. Preachers who do not have the good sense to see how exceptional are their illustrations (or instructions) can hardly expect practical people to have the poor judgment to accept them.

Inappropriate Humor

Some argue that we should never use humor in the pulpit. They rightly assume that preaching is a solemn task with eternal consequences. But this correct conclusion leads to instruction that is too strict if we do not recognize that matters are often expressed with the most power when they are expressed the most memorably. Humor is one way we can make people reflect on a truth in new and more serious ways. Jesus knew this when he proposed the preposterous images of people who carefully strain a gnat from their drink but then swallow a camel, or those who object to a splinter in another's eye while ignoring the log in their own. At times a touch of humor can drive home a point more aptly than plain statement. The truth remains serious but is related with levity that raises the hammer of thought and emotion to strike the heart with even greater impact.

Illustrative humor becomes inappropriate when it is merely decorative or derogatory. It seems a decree of our time that an address begin with a good joke. At sales seminars, professional meetings, social events, political functions, and sadly even in the pulpit, individuals feel they must begin with an anecdote. The rationale for this is that with a joke the speaker immediately wins the favor of an audience, establishes a friendly rapport, and proves that he or she has the ability to stave off boredom. Unfortunately, this type of introduction is so common that everyone in the audience is quite aware of why the humor is being used. If it has nothing to do with the content of the speech, the joke is patently manipulative and everyone knows it. Audiences may still laugh at the joke, but they automatically discredit a speaker who treats them with so little dignity. Preachers cannot afford such evaluations. If your anecdote does not press your point home, do not use it. Jokes for entertainment purposes alone have no place in the pulpit, not because they promote some great moral evil, but because glibness creates audience distrust.[27] Some well-known preachers draw crowds with their humor, but research indicates that when amusement quotients soar, persuasiveness nosedives. We love to watch a flimflam man conduct his medicine show, but only the foolish buy the medicine. When the healing is the Gospel we must not sell it so. William Cowper's poignant line ought still to prick our consciences: "'Tis pitiful to court a grin when you should win a soul."[28]

A preacher should not assume that because the congregation laughed, a joke performed its purpose. By its very nature humor is a sideways look at the world, often with an unusual perspective on foibles, frailties, and flaws in systems, institutions, and people. This makes some forms of humor exceedingly dangerous for the pastors called to minister to the weak and outcast of society. Laughter that grows out of disparagement of any person or group is fundamentally opposed to the Gospel. Though this instruction may seem obvious, it is easily obscured by the need many preachers feel to have the confirmation of audience approval that laughter seems to indicate. It is a great blessing that ethnic humor is now seen in most church circles for the offense it is. This was not always so. Illustration books for preachers printed early in this century by even the most forward thinking publishers were often filled with racist humor.[29] Today blatantly ethnic humor is at least viewed as being impolitic or impolite enough to have been banished from most pulpits. Less blatant forms of prejudice will also disappear when preachers recognize that where the race of an individual does not have consequence in an illustration, there are usually only prejudicial reasons for mentioning it.

Though ethnic humor is less prominent today, humor on the basis of gender, dialect, physical appearance, politics, and age remains sadly all too common among us. Preachers can easily fall into these humor traps. Too many preachers still punctuate anecdotes with phrases like, "You know how women are . . . "; or, "That's just like a woman to . . . "; or, "All the time my wife. . . ." Preachers who use such lines should not be so foolish as to believe they can then effectively minister to the females they have just ridiculed, even if the women laughed when the men did. Nor are men in times of distress likely to turn to pastors with a reputation for such insensitivity. No one really wants the counsel of someone who characteristically shames them or others.

The most benign stereotyping still hurts people and erodes ministry. Several years ago in a sermon I tried to convey the necessity of living a consistent Christian lifestyle to handle uncertain circumstances. To drive home the point about developing good Christian instincts, I told a popular account of an aging sheriff at a shooting range. He was trying to pass his annual marksmanship test but was having difficulty since he had just been fitted with a new pair of trifocals. I built up the humor of the sheriff's struggle as he moved back and forth, tilting his head up and down, attempting to get the distant target, the near front sights, and the nearer back sights of the pistol all in focus at the same time. Finally, I showed how his frustration grew so great that he gave up trying to get everything in focus, and let his years of training take over by instinctively shooting where he was certain the target had to be. The laughter told me the illustration had worked. But I regretted every titter and hated every guffaw when one of my dearest elders met me at the door afterwards with a new pair of trifocals on his nose. "Bryan," he said, "I never thought I would hear you make fun of old people." To the extent that anyone is treated without the dignity afforded them by God, the sermon fails even if the humor succeeds.

Often the most damaging illustrative insensitivities are directed at the pastor's own family. Some pastors seem never to tire of regaling the congregation with accounts of their wives' and children's embarrassments, fights, and flaws. Each week their families dutifully paste on a smile for the loved one making his reputation at their expense, but they often inwardly dread (and, in some cases, resent) the illustrations. I have made it a rule never to tell something about my wife or children (or others in the congregation) that could make them feel uncomfortable without telling the person involved what I plan to say, securing their permission to say it, and indicating to the congregation in the illustration that I have done so. Pastoral ministry is simply too important and too delicate for preachers to allow anyone to suspect them of gross insensitivity. As a healthy rule of thumb in all aspects of ministry, remember the only one at whom you can poke fun is yourself, and the only one you should not pat on the back is yourself.

Inappropriate Self-reference

You may appear to be patting yourself on the back if you are the occasional hero of your own illustrations or the too frequent focus of many of them. Such illustrations appear self-serving and undermine a congregation's confidence that the pastor has its best interests in view. Some instructors in previous generations forbade preachers to make any personal references in sermons.[30] This overreaction led to aloofness in preaching that denied people real access to the humanity of their pastor. Contemporary preaching has recovered the vital biblical teaching that listeners be able to identify with a preacher if they are to believe that the sermon has meaning for the realities of their lives (see 1 Cor. 9:22–23; 1 Thess. 2:8). But when preachers are the heroes of their own illustrations, this identification becomes impossible.

No one wants to identify with a braggart. I once heard a

minister begin an illustration by saying, "As you know, I have resolved never to go to bed without witnessing to at least one lost soul that day." He hardly had the words out of his mouth before the man in the pew behind me muttered under his breath, "Another notch on the gun belt for ol' Wyatt Earp." In this parishioner's mind, the pulpit broadcast of personal piety did not elevate regard for the pastor; it lowered him to the level of a swaggering, spiritual gunslinger. Preachers who want to tell of a personal spiritual success should be cautioned, at the least, to confess that the victory was a result of the Spirit working beyond their own weakness.[31]

Too much personal focus also can give illustrations, and the preacher using them, a bad name. Name-dropping one's noteworthy acquaintances in illustrations is a silly ploy for attention. Citing one's own accomplishments, degrees, or library acquisitions will undermine authority rather than establish esteem.[32] Preachers can also make their hobbies, personal interests, or families too frequently the object of their illustrations.[33] Lehman writes, "If, ministering to the same group of people, one consistently tells about himself, his wife, his children, his parents, his friends, and his dog, he may provoke a scream of resentment: 'Doesn't he ever talk about anything but himself and his family?' "[34] As has been indicated previously, the Bible, history, news accounts, the experiences of others, and personal experiences are all excellent sources for illustration. While accounts of personal experiences usually carry the most powerful audience identification characteristics, such illustrations must be balanced with material from other sources to avoid accusations of personal preoccupation. Every sermon does not need this balance, but the scope of a ministry does.

Another type of inappropriate self-reference occurs when the pastor begins to use the pulpit as a confessional. A confident vulnerability in which the pastor occasionally presents himself in difficult, awkward, or weak moments will help persons identify with the preacher and convince them that the Gospel is not only for Moses and his kin.[35] I never felt more failure as a minister than when a young mother prayed about my wife and me at a prayer meeting asking the Lord to bless us "even though they don't have problems like the rest of us." I knew then that the image I had been presenting to her was one of personal perfection that put the aid of the Gospel beyond her reach. The preacher's humanity is part of the message that illustrations should convey, but if a preacher too constantly illustrates with personal sin, weakness, and doubt, then the Gospel itself comes into question. People wonder what good the Gospel is if it cannot even help the preacher. Illustrations that present the pastor's own vulnerability should, at least, point to the victory the Gospel yet offers.

As is true of so many features of the ministry, the key to effective, nonoffending self-reference in the pulpit is balance. "The preacher's self-disclosures from the pulpit should reveal a balanced person."[36] Such a person is familiar enough with people not to be self-serving or self-preoccupied, familiar enough with life to acknowledge personal struggle, and familiar enough with the Gospel to indicate how it may help others because of where it has rescued the preacher himself.

Too Graphic

Illustrations are often the door through which unnecessarily graphic, sensational, or crude terms and images enter a sermon because preachers are willing to say almost anything to garner attention. Our open culture with its graphic entertainments desensitizes many to what is still offensive to ordinary and biblical sensibilities. Young couples today typically go together into the birthing room, but while vivid descriptions of the birth processes are perfectly acceptable conversation for the under-thirty set, they are highly offensive to the over-fifty crowd and frightening to children when mentioned from the pulpit.

Young preachers may be so calloused by the violence of modern movies that they do not recognize how gruesome or revolting their own illustrative descriptions can be. "Blood and guts" rarely has a place in the pulpit, and then only if the description has been carefully worded so as to minimize sensationalism and defend the sensitivities of the young, the old, and the squeamish.[37] The same is true of illustrations that contain suggestive sexual content. Stories may need to be presented differently in different situations regardless of their source. The story of David's sin with Bathsheba, for instance, should not be told in such a way as to pander to baser interests.[38] Sometimes the sources of such illustrations are problematic in themselves. While some people will tolerate an illustration from an R-rated movie or a best-selling scandal novel, others (parents, in particular) will understandably be upset that their pastor partakes of the very thing they caution their children against.[39] Preachers should always be mindful of what they may inadvertently endorse or expose by an illustration.

Sharing Confidences

Not only do illustrations unveil your innermost thoughts and activities, if you do not take special care, you may reveal the innermost thoughts and activities of those who have come to you for counsel. A ministry can be shattered in moments by revelations of matters disclosed in confidence.[40] Deane Kemper speaks strongly about this:

> One of the few absolutes in preaching is that there should be no stories from the pulpit out of the pastor's counseling ministry. Even if the incident goes back many years to a previous parish hundreds of miles away, with names and details altered, listeners will perceive parallels (real and imagined) to persons in the church or community and say to themselves (and later to others), "I know who that is." Even if no inferences are drawn (and they invariably are), the preacher who relates counseling experiences will find church members are reluctant to seek counsel from someone who is likely to turn their cases into sermon illustrations.[41]

This advice is well considered, and I have found it very valuable except in the absoluteness of its imperatives. I may well be wrong (these are extremely sensitive matters), but I believe you can on occasion use references to counseling situations if the identity of individuals involved is protected *and* you make it clear to the congregation that you are protecting the identity of the individuals. Particularly if the illustration shows how someone benefited from spiritual counsel, others experiencing similar problems may see they have cause for hope and seek similar counsel. If you indicate by the very way you tell the illustration that confidences will not be disclosed, then such seekers will know they need not fear preaching indiscretions.

One way I occasionally refer to counseling situations is by prefacing the illustrations with a sentence such as "A man came to my office a few years ago—I'll call him Bill." By saying, "I'll call him Bill," I tacitly announce to the congregation, "His name is not Bill, but for the purposes of protecting confidentiality, I want you to understand that I will refer to him by that name in this illustration." The same technique can be used in referring to other details of place, time, and problem. Having added this qualification, I heartily agree with Kemper that counseling illustrations that give people sufficient details to identify individuals (or think they can) will greatly damage our ministries and others' lives.

Distracting

Illustrations should promote a message's purpose, not distract from it. Sangster writes: "Odd as it may seem, some illustrations—some good illustrations—must be jettisoned by any man who would be a master of this craft. It is possible for an illustration to be too interesting, and too interesting *in itself*. The perfect illustration does its work, and exhausts its work in so doing."[42] Observing a few economizing guidelines will usually keep illustrations true to their purpose. Spurgeon cautions against illustrations that are intended to "dazzle" the listeners with multiple metaphors.[43] Dawson Bryan offers a little friendly satire on this advice by Spurgeon:

> Spurgeon has said concerning metaphorical illustrations: "THEY SHOULD NOT BE TOO NUMEROUS. . . . Some men seem never to have enough of metaphors; each one of their sentences must be a flower. They compass sea and land to find a fresh piece of colored glass for their windows. . . . Flowers upon the table at a banquet are well enough; but as nobody can live on banquets, they will become objects of contempt if they are set before us in lieu of substantial viands. The difference between a little salt with your meat and being compelled to empty the salt-cellar is clear to all." Here we have four metaphors in immediate succession to illustrate the principle of moderation in the use of metaphor—an admirable example of the violation of a principle in the very act of enforcing it.[44]

Let it suffice to say that the best illustrations are not so dense with the flowers of language that they cover the object they were meant to beautify.

The words of an illustration may be too high-flown or simply too numerous. Lived-body detail is needed; extraneous detail is not. An illustration can be too short if one denies it the narrative structure to distinguish it from an example, instance, allusion, or quote, but the preacher should not wax poetic over what could be crisply stated. Most of the time an illustration that goes over two or three paragraphs begins to belabor the point or steal attention from it. Illustrations are best kept short.[45] Word them efficiently with key terms of the biblical exposition interwoven in such a way as to lead the listener to the precise conclusion you want to make.

If the illustration neglects the key terms of the exposition, substitutes others, or clouds them in a flurry of new terms and images, listeners will wonder exactly what point you are trying to make. You should remember that listeners believe your illustration is about *the last thing said* before the illustration began. They do not expect the illustration to be about matters said two paragraphs earlier, or even two sentences earlier. The ear of a listener has a different reference point than the eye of a reader that can scan back over material previously presented. The terms of the illustration should act as a shaft of light illuminating the last thing said prior to the illustration's introduction (that may be a summary of much previous material), rather than having the listener pick his way through concepts in the diffuse light shining over distant or past materials.

Sometimes illustrations lead astray. The preacher gets caught up in the illustration and neglects the point actually being expounded. When the preacher must use an illustration to expound the illustration, obscurity rules. Ian MacPherson writes, "The lamp that burns so feebly that one has to light another lamp to see it is a pitifully poor illuminant."[46] More frequently hearers receive poor illustrative guidance when the preacher knows it is time to illustrate but has no good illustration to make the point. In desperation the minister chooses an old illustration that is near to the point, and as a result the congregation is treated to an interesting account that has absolutely nothing to do with the message at hand. It is better not to illustrate at all than to lead astray. To lead to an interpretation not supported by the details of an illustration only frustrates listeners and makes them doubt the preacher's competence.[47]

An illustration may distract from the point if you do not realize that the anecdote or image contains problems for the audience that detain their attention rather than leading them to an understanding of the point. You may endorse a source or may place individuals in a positive light who are highly offensive to the congregation. Elders who have fought a particular social or religious cause for years may be offended if their preacher cites material from an opposition periodical without comment.

If it is not the pastor's intention to challenge individuals' opinions with the illustration, congregational sensitivities and sensibilities must be kept in mind. A young minister preaching in Birmingham recently destroyed any possibility of having his sermon heard when he introduced an illustration by saying,

"When we defeated the forces of evil in the Civil War. . . ." Another pastor who told of being so "anxious to get to Florida on vacation that I drove 90 miles an hour for two hours straight," similarly lost a hearing for the point he was trying to make. Even if the illustration contains controversial concepts that are biblically defensible, if the sermon does not address the controversy directly, it is usually the better part of valor to postpone mention of the subject. It is unwise to stir up more snakes in an illustration than the sermon provides sticks to kill. Courage does not require one to say things in such a way that they cannot be heard.

Listeners have trouble tracking with the flow of a message when the illustrations are unresolved. A few years ago I spoke of visiting a young man in prison who had been convicted of murder in a drug feud. I had been told he became a Christian through his difficulties, but when I talked to him it became evident his "conversion" had been more of a legal ploy than a personal commitment. "I tried that religion stuff for a while," he said, "but it didn't do anything for me. So, I gave it up." After telling what the man said, I explained the need for selfless commitment to Christ if we are to know the true benefits of faith. I thought the sermon had gone rather well until I shook hands at the door and answered the question on every other person's lips: "Whatever happened to that young man you spoke to in prison?" I had not completed the plot I had introduced, thus leaving everyone focusing on that matter rather than on the subject of the sermon. Perhaps, by leaving the matter yet unresolved, the reader will note how tenaciously such lack of resolution tugs at the mind.

Worn Out

Most of the past masters of illustration advise against using books of stock illustrations.[48] Their concerns are well founded. Illustrations that come from dead or distant sources rarely have the timeliness, wording, or the present-world details that make them naturally fresh and compelling. A modern preacher who only seems capable of illustrating with archaisms about the blacksmith shop, steam engines, and puritan dress is an anachronistic joke. MacPherson appropriately comments:

> Antiquated anecdotes and stale stories of all kinds should be respectfully laid to rest. Having served their day and generation, it is high time they fell asleep. . . . Whenever, unmindful of its longevity and overfamiliarity, we are foolish enough to embark in the pulpit upon the telling of such a tale, the congregation tends to grow restive and weary, sharing no doubt in this regard the feelings of T. Harwood Pattison: "Who has not wished that Michelangelo had left the angel to slumber in the stone and not said a word about it?"[49]

Preaching is not an exercise in imitation and quotation.[50] God calls contemporary pastors with contemporary experiences to contemporary pulpits. If God had meant to call an individual from another time and place to your pulpit, he would have done so. Today's preachers should recognize the privileged uniqueness of their particular calling and honor it with the application of their own minds and experiences. The old preacher's adage still applies: "The cure for boredom is not brilliance; it is realism." Realism is hardly accessible if today's realities disappear from view whenever the pastor illustrates.

This does not mean we should never use old illustrations. Some classic illustrations reappear generation after generation because they are so apt. Bearded stories should not dominate a ministry, but this is no reason to throw away books of stock illustrations. The pastor who must weekly preach on Sunday morning and evening, teach a Sunday School class, lead Wednesday evening Bible study, give a talk at the Tuesday morning men's prayer breakfast, and regularly conduct funerals, weddings, and other special functions should feel no shame in using an illustration encyclopedia as a valuable resource in developing good messages. Only someone who does not maintain that kind of preaching schedule would berate a pastor for gleaning ideas from illustration books, periodical collections, computer listings, subscription services, anecdotes in *Reader's Digest,* the sermons and writings of well-known preachers, and any other ready resource that will help supply the ever-flowing fountain of needed illustrations.

The best preachers use illustration collections as tools rather than as direct sources. Instead of quoting an archaic or distant account directly, these master preachers use stock illustrations as catalysts for their own thought. They use their own experience to update the language, contemporize the situation, contextualize the events, omit irrelevant details, intensify the point, and heighten the climax. Occasionally the original illustration will be so aptly worded and constructed that it cannot be improved by such editing, but master preachers know that unless they are making a point of the illustration's history, such wholesale "lifting and pasting" should be rare.[51] Messages most consistently ignite other hearts when they are forged in the heart, mind, and reality of the one who delivers them.

Other cautions could be added here, and perhaps should be. However, this chapter on cautions could never be exhaustive enough to cancel every mistake caused by indiscretion, poor judgment, sloth, or sin. It is enough to remember that a good heart, a sound mind, a gentle spirit, and a genuine commitment to truth will cover a multitude of errors and create fine illustrations.

Notes

1. Westminster Confession of Faith, I.v.
2. Edward F. Marquart, *Quest for Better Preaching* (Minneapolis: Augsburg, 1985), p. 153.
3. Dawson C. Bryan, *The Art of Illustrating Sermons* (Nashville: Cokesbury, 1938), p. 172; J. Daniel Baumann, *An Introduction to Contemporary Preaching* (Grand Rapids: Baker, 1972), p. 180.
4. Bryan, *The Art of Illustrating Sermons,* pp. 173–74.
5. Ralph L. Lewis with Gregg Lewis, *Inductive Preaching: Helping People Listen* (Westchester, Ill.: Crossway, 1983), p. 82.

6. Charles Haddon Spurgeon, *The Art of Illustration*, Third Series of *Lectures to My Students* (London: Marshall Brothers., 1922) pp. 4–5.
7. *Westminster Larger Catechism*, Q. and A. 159.
8. R. F. Horton, *The Word of God* (London: T. Fisher Unwin, 1898), pp. 284–85.
9. Spurgeon, *The Art of Illustration*, p. 8.
10. John Killinger, *Fundamentals of Preaching* (Philadelphia: Fortress, 1985), pp. 30–31.
11. R. E. O. White, *A Guide to Preachers* (Grand Rapids: Eerdmans, 1973), p. 171.
12. Lewis, *Inductive Preaching*, p. 157.
13. Deane A. Kemper, *Effective Preaching* (Philadelphia: Westminster, 1985), p. 81; see also, Lewis, *Inductive Preaching*, p. 37.
14. Ian MacPherson, *The Art of Illustrating Sermons* (Nashville: Abingdon, 1964), p. 38.
15. J. Daniel Baumann, *An Introduction to Contemporary Preaching*, p. 172.
16. John Killinger, *Fundamentals of Preaching*, p. 109.
17. MacPherson, *The Art of Illustrating Sermons*, pp. 17–18.
18. Louis Paul Lehman, *Put a Door on It* (Grand Rapids: Kregel, 1975), p. 39.
19. W. E. Sangster, *The Craft of Sermon Illustration* (London: Epworth, 1948), p. 91.
20. Henry H. Mitchell, *The Recovery of Preaching* (San Francisco: Harper and Row, 1977), p. 157.
21. Sangster, *The Craft of Sermon Illustration*, p. 90.
22. Thomas V. Liske, *Effective Preaching* (New York: McMillan, 1960), p. 200.
23. Ibid., p. 199.
24. MacPherson, *The Art of Illustrating Sermons*, pp. 178–79.
25. Lehman, *Put a Door on It*, pp. 72–73.
26. Baumann, *An Introduction to Contemporary Preaching*, p. 180.
27. Ralph Lewis, *Speech for Persuasive Preaching* (Wilmore, Ky.: Ralph Lewis, 1968), p. 95.
28. From "The Task," by William Cowper.
29. See, for example, *Cyclopedia of Religious Anecdotes*, comp. James Gilchrist Lawson (Chicago: Revell, 1923).
30. Killinger, *Fundamentals of Preaching*, p. 31.
31. Ilion T. Jones, *Principles and Practice of Preaching* (New York: Abingdon, 1956), p. 142.
32. Kemper, *Effective Preaching*, p. 89.
33. Sangster, *The Craft of Sermon Illustration*, p. 84.
34. Lehman, *Put a Door on It*, p. 74.

35. Killinger, *Fundamentals of Preaching*, p. 31.
36. Kemper, *Effective Preaching*, p. 89.
37. Liske, *Effective Preaching*, p. 199.
38. James Cox, *Preaching: A Comprehensive Approach to the Design and Delivery of Sermons* (New York: Harper and Row, 1985), p. 162.
39. Kemper, *Effective Preaching*, p. 86.
40. Killinger, *Fundamentals of Preaching*, p. 119.
41. Kemper, *Effective Preaching*, p. 88.
42. Sangster, *The Craft of Sermon Illustration*, p. 96.
43. Spurgeon, *The Art of Illustration*, p. 9.
44. Bryan, *The Art of Illustrating Sermons*, p. 175.
45. Baumann, *An Introduction to Contemporary Preaching*, p. 180.
46. MacPherson, *The Art of Illustrating Sermons*, p. 179.
47. Lehman, *Put a Door on It*, p. 95.
48. William Evans, *How to Prepare Sermons and Gospel Addresses* (Chicago: The Bible Institute Colportage Assoc., 1913), p. 143.
49. MacPherson, *The Art of Illustrating Sermons*, pp. 164–65.
50. Joseph Ruggles Wilson, "In What Sense Are Preachers to Preach Themselves?" *Southern Presbyterian Review* 25 (July 1874), p. 355.
51. Bryan, *The Art of Illustrating Sermons*, p. 201.

Chapter 9

Finding and Filing Illustrations

FINDING THEM

As we have seen, preachers get illustrations from several basic sources: personal experiences (read about, heard from others, or personally lived), news accounts, historical accounts, literary materials, imagination, and the Bible. How the preacher finds illustrations is no mystery, but it does require some discipline. As was mentioned in chapter 5, a preacher's daily experience with all these sources creates a passing parade of illustrations, even though the parade may not be obvious to others (and even though starting preachers may fear they will never be able to see the parade).[1] You see the parade with a trained eye. Such an eye develops the more you preach, and the more your daily being becomes oriented toward ministry. Seeing illustrations around you is a constant challenge that becomes a lifestyle.[2] As the metamorphosis occurs from private parishioner who consumes sermons to pulpit servant who prepares sermons, you will naturally develop the skill of seeing illustrations if you are convinced of the importance of doing so and do not too early fall into the habit of only using the illustrations of others.

Finding illustrations is like finding geodes in a creek bottom. The special rocks are all around, but it takes finding a few of the crystals yourself before your eye begins to recognize the shape and texture of the rocks that hold the sparkling treasure within. Unless you walk the creek to find the geodes, all you will see in any creek bottom is an endless supply of indistinguishable, useless pebbles. But once you train your eye, beautiful treasures abound in this most ordinary of worlds.[3] The treasures lie in the open for all eyes to see, but only the practiced eye sees them. After a little experience most preachers discover the delight of finding illustrative treasures right under the noses of their people. The gems are somehow all the more special when they come from a place where everyone could have seen them but do not. People in the pew also appreciate these illustrations because they help all recognize the beauty and meaning their own world holds. The preacher's eye truly is special. By seeing *what* others see, but not *as* others see, your vision enables people to appreciate their own world more for the biblical truths it discloses.

KEEPING THEM

Often illustrations will come to mind as you prepare a message. If the point to be made is sharply defined, the impact of the truth will often throw mental sparks against a memory or recent experience, and the illustration immediately flames into light. However, most preachers will be seriously handicapped if they only rely upon immediate inspiration for sermon illustrations. Most of us find we must combine illustrations that we have stored for use with those that spring to mind when we prepare our messages. Through the centuries of homiletical instruction a number of "systems" have been devised to help preachers save and retrieve the illustrations they discover. Computer programs and subscription services are only recent innovations in a much developed field. No one system is right for everyone, and rather than trying to evaluate all the systems in use, a few guidelines will probably be sufficient to help you develop a personally appropriate method. '

Do Something

Almost any system of collecting and filing illustrations is better than no system at all. Perhaps the only exception is a system that is so complicated that it becomes a barrier to the preacher developing original illustrations. Filing illustrations will require some discipline, and there is no sense in adding unnecessary layers of complication to it. If you cannot file your illustrations in a matter of seconds your system will probably wear you out and quickly fall into disuse. On the other hand, if you have no storage and retrieval system, you will find yourself too frequently delving into the shopworn columns of the illustration manuals or falling back on illustrations used in previous messages. As a result, your messages can begin to sound impersonal, or worse, unthoughtful.

Prepare Early

No filing system is more important or more basic than knowing well ahead of time what your subject and/or text will be. Having the subject or the text in hand some weeks prior to preaching a message is like having a powerful magnet for pertinent ideas and illustrations. This does not mean that you should have the entire sermon in hand weeks before it is preached. For most of us this is simply impossible, and even if it were possible, such a practice might rob messages of their spontaneous fire. Still, by knowing generally what a sermon will be about, the preacher can begin to collect, sort, and evaluate illustrations long before they are actually needed.

Often preachers keep a letter-size file with a separate folder for each sermon planned for upcoming weeks or months. Then as an illustration occurs to them or they come across an article dealing with the subject, they simply drop the material into the appropriate folder so that they have a healthy reservoir of ideas on hand for the week the sermon must be fully prepared. Not only will illustrations find their way into such a file, but potential outlines, exegetical discoveries, applicational thoughts, and expositional ideas are also drawn to the magnet of a "presermon file." You certainly do not have to use all the material collected in such a file. Often there will be more materials than you can use. However, even if you use very little of the file for a particular message, over time such a system will undoubtedly develop a ministry with higher quality sermons than the all too typical Friday-afternoon-flurry and Saturday-night-frenzy.

A presermon file is the most basic way of filing and retrieving illustrations. No one should debate that it may be better to have file cabinets or computer databases with illustrations carefully alphabetized, topically arranged, and cross-referenced to texts. But few preachers seem to have the time actually to set up and to manage such systems. A presermon file is a manageable fall-back position for almost any preacher. The system takes minimal effort and time. Still, it allows the preacher to retrieve illustrations from more sources than anecdote manuals or faulty memories under the pressure of immediate performance. And by helping you apply some minimal thought and planning to future messages, the overall quality of your sermons will steadily improve.

Write Them Down—Now!

No filing system will work if you have nothing to put in it. It is important when you come across an illustration that you write it down immediately. It is just as important that you write it down with sufficient detail that you can remember what it is about. Every pastor has faced the limitations of memory in moments of great pain such as, "I had a great illustration for this yesterday, but what was it?" Most preachers who determine to "write it down later" had best simply resign themselves to forgetting 90 percent of their potential illustrations.

Many great communicators have disciplined themselves to carry a notebook in their wallets or shirt pockets in order to record immediately illustrations and other thoughts pertinent to their messages. Of course, it will do no good to carry such a notebook if, a month later, or whenever you are ready to add the illustration to a file, the note is so brief that you cannot remember the illustration. In recent years I have kept a small tablet of "stick 'em" notes in my wallet. That way I always have paper to jot down an illustration. In addition, I try to write the illustration and its point down fully enough that, instead of having to type those notes on another card, I simply stick the note on a three by five-inch card and file it in an appropriate presermon or other file (see below). This way, once I write it down, I do not have to struggle to remember an illustration I ran across days ago, nor do I have to worry about when I will get the time to transfer my wallet notes to a more complete form for filing.

If I can save myself the bother of writing anything down, I will do so. My family has long insisted that I be the last to read the daily paper, since when I do, sections tend to get savaged by my scissors. I read magazines with scissors in hand and books with a highlighter in reach. That which cannot be clipped I photocopy, or I jot down enough information in my wallet notes that I can remember and retrieve the illustration when I need it. Then I file the clipping, photocopy, or wallet note with other illustrations. My illustration files may not be pretty, but then I am not trying to publish them. I am the only one who has to look at them, and I know that if I make my work unnecessarily difficult, I am not likely to continue it.

File Them

What do you do with good illustrations that do not have a place in your presermon file or have already been used? File them.[4] As bothersome as it may be to set them up initially, illustration files are of immense value to preachers who need material for weekly messages. Such files can save preachers huge amounts of time and energy while dramatically improving the quality of their sermons.

Topic Files

While some preachers may prefer to develop their own topical system for cataloging their illustrations, you can save yourself much work by purchasing one of the good topical catalogs on the market today. You can always add or delete categories according to personal preferences and changing interests without having to "reinvent the wheel" of a comprehensive cataloging system that typically is broken into two hundred or more categories. Some preachers simply alphabetize their illustrations. Others catalog according to the Dewey decimal system. Currently, I prefer to file my illustrations in a three by five-inch card system marketed by a major publisher. The file readily accepts the wallet notes described above, and I can easily change the topic categories by inserting or deleting tab cards. If I am undecided about which topic category an illustration best fits, or if I think it fits very well in a number of categories, I simply make photocopies and file the illustration in each of the appropriate categories.

Computer cataloging systems are also very adaptable, and some have high-powered topical search and cross-reference programs (often these can be updated monthly through various subscription services). Typically computer illustrations may be placed directly into a sermon manuscript using standard word processing software. The only drawback to computer cataloging is the time needed to input original illustrations that are not part of the original or subscription packages. However, it is easier to file duplicate copies of the illustration in multiple topic and text categories using computer processing. If I did not depend so much on my wallet notes, I would probably prefer a computerized retrieval system. Evaluate your own practices, needs, and budget to help you determine which system will best serve your own personal needs and style.

Two systems frequently used by pastors (and just as frequently abandoned) should be cautioned against. Pasting illustrations in books and piling illustrations in "shoeboxes" without a topical key of some sort is an exercise in futility. Once the collection is of any real size, so much must be read or scanned to find the right illustration that preachers soon find they cannot afford the time to use their own files. A system too sparing on organization is just as frustrating as one too complex.

Two other cautions can be mentioned briefly. Frequently topical catalogs fail to include categories for special occasions, the church calendar, or holidays. Because so many messages must be developed by the preacher with just such events in mind, it is important not to add these categories to every illustration file. Next, remember an illustration file is not the only topical file a preacher should keep. Haddon Robinson wisely advises a letter-sized file for topics or texts the preacher will frequently address. Such a file can hold notes, brochures, booklets, articles, past sermons or messages from others, photocopies, and much more information that will be irrevocably lost if the pastor takes no care in storing it for future reference.[5]

Text Files

Some of the illustration encyclopedias on the market list biblical texts that certain of their stock illustrations are likely to fit. Although sometimes the fit seems stretched, the mass appeal of these cross-referencing systems indicates how helpful it is for preachers to have their illustrations keyed to texts as well as topics. Personal cross-referencing can be accomplished by making a notation in a notebook of texts when particularly apt illustrations are placed in the card file, or by purchasing computer software that allows one to note texts that are served by particular illustrations as they are entered into the database.

Some preachers even keep a separate file cataloged by texts and deposit illustrations directly into the file. Leslie Flynn describes his text file this way:

> The second of my major file sections is the textual or biblical drawer. I have a folder for every small Old Testament book and several folders for the longer books. Only for Genesis do I have a folder for every chapter.
>
> For the New Testament I have a folder for every chapter from Acts to Revelation. Any illustration that alluded to the story of the Philippian jail would be filed under Acts 16.
>
> I handle the Gospels differently. For Matthew, Mark, Luke, and John I follow Robertson's *Harmony of the Gospels* with his chronological breakdown into 184 sections. This enables me to file in one place all material on any event recorded in more than one Gospel.[6]

The reason to have a text file of some sort should be obvious. Some companies market commentaries with the promise that they have an illustration for every major text. It can almost make you breathless to think of developing a file that contains many illustrations for a text before you have even begun your sermon preparation.

Just Do It

Hardly anyone argues against having a good illustration file. Almost everyone struggles to develop and maintain one. If the struggle is too much, then preachers should at least develop a presermon file. Some may wish they had developed a better filing system for their illustrations years ago but now feel it would just be too much work with too little return to get such a system together. However, if you start with an economical product on the market, customize it by adding a few personal categories, and then add only two new illustrations per week, you will soon have a highly personal and extremely useful file. Yes, developing an extensive, personalized illustration file takes some time. But though the best time to have planted a tree was twenty-five years ago, the second best time is now.

Notes

1. Ian MacPherson, *The Art of Illustrating Sermons* (Nashville: Abingdon, 1964), p. 25.
2. R. E. O. White, *A Guide to Preaching* (Grand Rapids: Eerdmans, 1973), p. 173.
3. Thomas V. Liske, *Effective Preaching* (New York: Macmillan, 1960), p. 183.
4. Excellent discussions of this topic are found in Haddon Robinson, *Biblical Preaching: The Development and Delivery of Expository Messages* (Grand Rapids: Baker, 1980), p. 154; Leslie B. Flynn, *Come Alive with Illustrations: How to Find, Use, and File Good Stories for Sermons and Speeches* (Grand Rapids: Baker, 1987), pp. 103–9.
5. Robinson, *Biblical Preaching*, p. 154.
6. Flynn, *Come Alive with Illustrations*, pp. 106–7.

Tell Me a Story

Once upon a time there was a preacher who traveled to many churches across his land with messages about Jesus and his Word. The people of the land greatly appreciated the preacher when he spoke in their churches. They said, "We understand what he says. He doesn't just know about the Bible. He sounds as if he really knows what we face every day, and he shows us how Scripture really applies to our lives."[1] As the people's appreciation of him grew, so did the preacher's reputation. This, of course, led other preachers (some with godly motives, some with other motives) to want to find out what was making this man so effective. The ministers invited the traveling preacher to a conference to teach them his "technique." The preacher came to the conference, but instead of teaching something novel, he talked to the ministers about Jesus' method of teaching truths with parables. With a story or two of his own, the preacher encouraged the other ministers to speak so that they could be heard and understood, rather than to strive for great oratory in their preaching. "It is better for the message to be understood than for the messenger to be worshiped," he said.

In the question-and-answer period after the seminar, a minister rose to his feet to ask a question. With genuine perplexity he said, "I went to seminary with you. I know you are a man of great intelligence and that you know deep truths which I do not. But it seems to me, you are not being fair to your own gifts when you put so much emphasis on illustration. You always preach with stories. Why not simply state what Scripture teaches? Shouldn't we just present truth as truth?"

The preacher thought for a moment before responding and then smiled. "To answer," he said, "let me tell you a story."

He began, "One day Bare Truth came walking into town. What he had to say was very important, but he looked very intimidating with bulging muscles and hard knuckles. Some people remembered when he had hurt them before. As a result, most people went into their houses to wait for Bare Truth to finish his business. Only the strongest of the townspeople did not mind Bare Truth's visits.

"The next day Parable came to town. He looked just like most of the town's people and dressed in ordinary clothes, but he told of all the places he had been and the sights he had seen. All the people loved to visit with Parable. They came out to greet him and invited him into their homes. 'Come in and have a cup of coffee and a piece of pie,' many offered.

"Bare Truth was upset that Parable got a reception so unlike his own. He went to the other town visitor and said, 'Tell me, Parable, why do people greet you with such warmth when I am Truth they should hear?'

"Instead of answering, Parable took off his hat and jacket and put them on Bare Truth. Truth was transformed. He was no less strong. He was no less Truth. But the people saw him in an entirely different light. When he put on Parable's clothes, Truth showed he really was concerned that the people hear him. When the people recognized that Truth cared enough about them to find out what he needed to do to have them listen to him, they listened all the more intently. The very people who had invited Parable for coffee and donuts, now invited Truth, too.

"To this day, when Truth has business in town, he puts on Parable's clothes so that the people will hear him and deal with him."

Notes

1. Adapted from a story told by Annette Harrison in "Tell Me a Story," by Joseph Schuster in *St. Louis Home* (May 1989), pp. 17–18.

Communication Theory Contributions

THE IMPACT OF NARRATIVE

Because life-situation illustrations are usually brief stories, we need to think more about how narratives communicate meaning and values. More and more research indicates that communities of all types require the sharing of narratives for individuals to communicate and to function together as a social unit. Without such narratives, the meaning of words quickly shifts, fragments, or disintegrates. Narratives both supplement communication and maintain its viability and effectiveness. This dynamic is true not only for general communication, but also for communication of spiritual matters.

Whether we realize it or not, all of us by nature encourage others to *experience* meanings whenever we want them to understand our words. For instance, when our child asks us what "stealing" means, we are not likely to go to a dictionary, although we can find precise definitions there. We are more likely to explain narratively. We say, "If you had a new bicycle and a mean boy came along and took it away from you, that would be stealing." The narrative is simple but comprehensive. The account contains logical definition, but by allowing the child to experience the lived-body reality of the concept, we also allow him or her to understand at a level that mere propositional definition cannot touch. The story acts as an experiential dictionary to define the word's meaning.[1] The concreteness within the imaginative experience allows the child to understand in terms of his or her own world. While the meaning of the concept is not entirely revealed by the brief narrative, the account acts as a foundation on which meanings can be built, understood, and interrelated.

What we intuitively consider effective communication for children can be a model of what serves for effective communication to everyone. Since lived-body experiences translate meaning for individuals, framing those experiences in narrative gives others access to the same meaning. In other words, stories are much more than entertainment; they are a means of communicating truth in a way it can be more fully understood.

Preachers who understand these narrative dynamics have a tremendous advantage in making the language of the pulpit the living Word among God's people through illustration.[2] They realize that before their listeners can fully comprehend what they are trying to get across in their sermons, the listeners must participate in the same type of experience that originally communicated meaning to the speaker. That is why narratives must be included in preaching. In a sermon, descriptions of such experiences have a beginning and an end; are set off in time or have some duration; require the involvement of individuals either as participants or perceivers; occur within spatial and/or contextual references; and require development of thought, objects, or persons—that is, they have an implicit narrative structure.

HISTORICAL USES OF NARRATIVE

Traditional studies often sought to reduce communication to its linguistic essences. Yet most theorists today acknowledge that communication cannot be reduced to mere words, propositions, sentences, or syntax. Space, time, and relational dynamics always participate in conveying meaning. Their features work together with the words and syntax to constitute the story behind everything that is communicated.

Classic Narrative Dynamics

The concept of the irreducibility of communication to grammar, definitions, and syntax is an old one. The thought glimmers even in ancient Greece. Aristotle writes, "We are most strongly convinced when we suppose anything to have been demonstrated."[3] His concept of "demonstration" reflects various types of proofs, but implicit in Aristotle's communication paradigm is the basic assumption of modern communication research that a concept assumes plausibility, power, and persuasiveness because the listener recognizes its validity through experiencing it. This is especially evident when a speaker uses an "example." "Examples function like witnesses," says Aristotle.[4] He goes so far as to conclude that induction (i.e., using examples to support logical conclusions) is the basis of all reasoning.[5] For this most significant of ancient communication theorists, encapsulating elements of human experience and accompanying them with logic undergirds all shared thought.

Of special interest to preachers is Aristotle's discussion of how speakers must persuade when presenting matters that have no absolute logical proofs. In such cases, Aristotle argues, experiential dynamics play an even more critical role. Speakers extend "premises" to listeners who draw conclusions based upon their full range of experience with similar ideas or occurrences. Listeners use their own pasts to create significance or assign probable meanings for the words and arguments the speaker uses. As a result, effective speakers use premises that presume or provide some associated experience for the audience. In this way the listeners can (1) recognize the probability of the premise, (2) associate the premise with other related matters in past experience, (3) identify the premise by historical or invented examples, and (4) inductively extrapolate general conclusions from those particulars.[6] In other words, for example, while preachers may not be able to demonstrate categorically that adultery destroys families or that materialism leads to despair, they can illustrate these maxims by narratives, knowing that listeners will more likely accept conclusions within their own framework of reference. Narrative assumes the weight of the persuasive load in these messages.

Even when communication studies concentrate on words in themselves, narrative dynamics cannot be ignored. The link between experience and meaning in communication is especially evident in metaphors, the fundamental building blocks of all language.[7] Metaphors make something understandable by ascribing to it characteristics of something familiar. If both elements of the metaphor are familiar, the focus is on the relationship between them. Regardless of the precise mechanism of comparison, however, the metaphor cannot work if some element of the figure of speech is not already familiar to the listener. In other words, the path to understanding leads back to the experience. Meaning is conveyed by the matrix of events, sensations, and persons—i.e., the story—that references the words.[8]

Neo-Classical Narrative Dynamics

The experiential tenets underlying ancient communication theories reemerged and were refined early in the twentieth century. In his "Context Theorem of Meaning," I. A. Richards writes that the meaning of a word is defined in two ways: setting and context. The words that surround a word and the ways people use the word (i.e., syntax and usage) constitute its "setting."[9] But more important to preaching is Richards' insight into the second source of meaning. He says all words—all expressions—convey meaning through a mental process in which a person scans past experiences for associations that form the "context"[10] of the words. With this definition of "context" Richards incorporates Aristotle's thought and moves beyond it.

If all communication relies on present comparisons with past incidents, then the supposed power that words have in themselves dies.[11] Traditional notions of linguistic logic and proposition-oriented communication dissolves. Words only signal references to experiences, and their meaning lies in fitting words into the context of life whose instances are the references for those words.[12] Thus words are not disparate thought units syntactically connected for meaning; they are parts of contexts whose usage is ever eliciting consideration of the experiences that hold meaning.

Context not only acts as the field in which a word's meaning is found, it also identifies the horizon of possible meanings an individual can consider. The less familiar or concrete a concept, the more contexts must be relied upon for defining its horizons. Thus, the more abstract a concept, the more contexts must be added to define a specific meaning.[13] "And this is the more true," writes Richards, "the more severe and abstract the philosophy is. As it grows more abstract we think increasingly by means of metaphors we profess not to be relying on."[14]

Preachers may believe that because what they are saying is doctrinally profound that it needs little experiential reference. Actually, the more lofty the expressions, the more they must be "earthed" to have any real meaning. Spiritual abstractions require more experiential contexts than those abstractions whose meaning is closely tied to ordinary experience. Simple messages *have* experiential analogies; difficult messages *need* them. Narratives that contain and create these experiential references are always pertinent.

MODERN USES OF NARRATIVE

Kenneth Burke further exposes the experiential foundations of communication. His work more than any other has led later researchers to consider the narrative structures supporting everything we say. In Burke the loose connections between word meaning and narrative extracted from previous theorists' presuppositions are drawn so taut that the significance of narrative practically bursts into view.

A key thought for Burke is that words and symbols are inherently defined by what they are not—"everything is its other."[15] He derives this seemingly absurd conclusion from the common sense observation that things are defined by their "substance." In a virtual pun analysis Burke shows that quite literally "a thing's sub-stance would be something that stands beneath or supports the person or thing."[16] Such an analysis inevitably places meaning in a thing's context rather than in the thing itself. A word or symbol is defined by the very process of pointing to the things that are outside of itself. Any word or symbol, therefore, is essentially synecdochic (i.e., the part standing for the whole context).[17]

Narrative Drama

In Burke's thinking, similar to the analysis of I. A. Richards, any term is defined by the "contexts of situations" in which it is found.[18] Burke furthers the analysis, though, by identifying those elements that comprise the contexts of situations: "what was done (act), when or where it was done (scene), who did it (agent), how he did it (agency), and why (purpose)."[19] Burke's own term for the use of this theatrical sounding analysis of the contexts of communication is "dramatism." Dramatism contends we must seize meaning from the interplay of persons, places, and events mingling within and without any given expression. It is not Burke's choice to label this analysis "storyism," but "dramatism" so echoes story features that its dynamics cannot help but underscore the narrative mechanism at work in the communication process. An utterance communicates by the story features that surround and permeate its expression. Meaning is communicated not merely by comparisons to past contexts, but by the dynamics— the drama—of the current situation.

The story of an expression yields its meaning. Words point to contexts, situations, and characters beyond themselves. They are imbedded in the story of the events around them. Thus, illustration of some form cannot be avoided when we express anything. Illustrative contexts must either be provided by the speaker or conjured into consideration by the listener for words to have significance. Words disclose stories, but simultaneously narratives clothe words.[20]

The Meaning of Narrative

Walter Fisher uses Burke to show how narrative pervades all our communication.[21] First, Fisher demonstrates that the elements of dramatism are narrative features. Then he integrates the Burkean concept of "identification" into the narrative model. Burke argues that communication can occur only if speaker and listener become "consubstantial"; i.e., they identify with each other by sharing "common sensations, concepts, images, ideas, attitudes" (cf. 1 Cor. 9:19–22).[22] When he sees that we convey meaning with narrative elements with which we and others can identify, Fisher concludes effective communication occurs only through shared stories.

Fisher is not arguing that narrative is simply another communication device. Narration is "the master metaphor." It subsumes all other communication models and methods.[23] Narrative is essential to understanding one's own place in life and to creating the means for individuals to act and to think in concert. Fisher applies this premise to ordinary experience, communication of even the most technical nature, ethics of all sorts, social organization and conduct, and religion.[24] Narratives enable us to know who we are, what others communicate, and what God communicates.

The Means of Narrative

Fisher explains what stories do, but the question remains of how we can use them. For this we turn to Rolf von

Eckartsberg. In delving for access to the deep recesses of the human psyche this social psychologist discovered the word barrier that communication theorists had confronted in parallel studies: Words alone are not enough to discover or disclose the meanings veiled in the psyche and past experience. In his search for another route into the depths of others' thought processes, von Eckartsberg discerned how to use narrative as a tool, as well as a map.

Echoing others, von Eckartsberg writes, "Our being entangled and intertwined in stories is our most primordial social reality experience. It is the foundation of social meaning. On the basis of these shared stories . . . our social life becomes comprehensible."[25] But how do we use this information? He gives the following answer: "If we are to ascertain and interpret the culture-building acts of individuals we have to find a way to these realities and to give them some form of expression or inscription. We have to get descriptions of such existential events. We have to collect life-stories."[26] Because our being entangled and intertwined in stories is how we understand ourselves and each other, von Eckartsberg realizes such stories are fundamental communication tools. They give us access to experiences where meaning resides that we can share with others. "These stories constitute life-texts."[27] By collecting and recounting the stories of others, "we can learn from their example, from their success and failure."[28]

Under this analysis stories are not merely a way of describing communication structures; they are tools by which we most fully comprehend each other. Through stories we have the best opportunity for understanding what other people's lives and words are about. "We find ourselves caught up and moved by the events and personages of the story. We live through their life with them in sympathetic response."[29] Our experience is vicarious, but it situates our lived-body consciousness in the experience of another, creating highly efficient, effective, and accurate communication.[30]

Shared stories function as cultural dictionaries. They are the experiential referents that guide personal understanding by defining society's value and coding its communication in narrative contexts. This insight brings communication thought full circle. For almost twenty centuries the tradition stemming from Aristotle sought to determine how human experience could be reduced to its propositional essence. Now there is a growing consensus that such reductions are impossible or, at least, impaired. Texts and speech that use experience (rather than eliminating it) communicate best. What was thought to be efficient is simply not effective in communicating the full depth and scope of meanings we ordinarily require for true understanding of ourselves, our world, and others.

PREACHING USES OF NARRATIVE

While such a perspective does not discard the use of propositional statements in preaching,[31] it no longer allows narrative elements to be considered merely ancillary to the propositions being communicated. The instruction is therefore clear: stories not only beacon implicitly behind all communication, they should be used explicitly in communication. This premise applies to speaking situations in general and to preaching in specific.[32]

Bridging the Abyss

In terms reflective of the speech theorists, Reuel Howe insightfully observes that the preacher's sermons "are only a preliminary contribution to the sermons which are formed in each hearer as he responds out of his meanings to the meanings of the preacher."[33] Such a perspective immediately dispels the notion that listeners are passively waiting to receive and consume whatever the preacher dishes out. If the listeners understand anything, it is because they are actively translating the preacher's words through their own experience. They are partners with him in the preaching task, or there is no communication.

This dynamic immediately creates problems. Henry Eggold writes:

> Both the preacher and the hearer bring to the sermon their understanding of their religious tradition and contemporary life. And already trouble stalks, because the preacher's understanding of the religious tradition is probably deeper than the layman's; and, conversely, the layman's understanding of contemporary life is probably broader than the preacher's.[34]

Add to these disparate experiential dynamics the commonly accepted barriers to religious communication—language and image discrepancies; educational, sexual, and cultural differences; anxieties, tensions, and defensiveness—and the preaching partnership seems a tenuous arrangement at best. The distance between pulpit and pew seems better characterized as an abyss rather than an aisle.

For listeners to understand fully what preachers mean, the listeners must reach some consensus of meanings and values with them. To do this ideally, a utopian world would be required. In this world listeners would experience the very things that inform the preacher's thought in order to compensate for the differences and defenses that, ultimately, make each individual's thought separate and unique. Such a utopia is inaccessible. Still, communication can occur. How? By letting listeners vicariously experience the events or accounts that framed the preacher's thought or by formulating an account that provides common ground for understanding. By relating life-situation illustrations the preacher creates the aural environment of his thought, thereby translating listeners to that world in which they can live through meanings with him.

Closing the Circle

There is a natural bending toward the other person in effective communication as "I turn toward you, and you, in turn, focus on me," in order that we may penetrate each other's thoughts and capture each other's words.[35] These dynamics are masterfully captured by Morris Niedenthal and Charles Rice as they relate preaching to narrative communication:

> See the storyteller in the middle of a circle of people; by the lake or around the fire; at the supper table on the evening of the funeral, over food gone cold and dishes unwashed; one to one, as the story comes out for the first, the healing time; over breakfast, with the newspaper open, remembering a little girl or boy; on the Fourth of July at a picnic, or at home on a snowy day with your grandparents; in a foxhole or a bar, or at the family reunion or around the communion table. The opening line is liturgical, a call to enter in and let something happen: "Once upon a time . . ." or "I remember when . . ." or "I've never told you this but . . ." or "A certain man had two sons. . . ." Wherever it happens and whatever the form, we recognize it immediately, and we begin, as W. B. Gallie has said, to follow, to go with the story and the storyteller, whether the story is unfamiliar or one we have heard a thousand times.
>
> When the signal is given we know—and the knowing is simply a matter of being human—that this is not the time to question, to analyze, to do anything. It is a time to lean forward, to enter in, to let ourselves be moved along, to follow. . . .
>
> The storyteller and the circle of listeners bend to each other. There is in the very nature of storytelling a posture, a leaning forward. And this is true of both the listener and the storyteller, as if the story cannot be told without this attentive bending to each other.[36]

Biblical preaching reflects the principles evident in this scene. Biblical narratives are structured to accommodate the recounting of truths around ten thousand campfires, across a hundred million kitchen tables, and through countless generations. Those who preach the Bible should not cavalierly bypass the instruction its structures provide. Preaching is the sharing of stories—not necessarily fantasies, fairy tales, or fictions—but the accounts that tell us our place in the world, the things we value, and the priorities that must govern our relationships.

Authentic Uses of Narrative

Preachers want to be heard and understood. It is simply not enough for a message to sound religious. Preachers want messages that traverse the pulpit-pew abyss and live in the minds of believers in order to transform hearts. Such messages must have ingredients that make them acceptable for public address and translatable to other minds. Stories are uniquely qualified to serve both functions because narratives serve the needs that underlie effective preaching and frame the thought that communicates understanding. Seen from this communication perspective, the telling of stories is not mere entertainment or tension relief in preaching; it is a primary mode of explanation and application. If preachers never uncover the stories that communicate in the way we all live and learn, there is the danger that religious professionals will more and more become the guardians of a linguistic orthodoxy to which all assent, but which few understand, and fewer live.

These conclusions point toward the need for a more authentic preaching: that which moves from abstract propositions to dialogue on "what happened to me last week" or "what has happened to someone who is typical of us." Such preaching may seem less erudite, even less literate, but nonetheless, it approaches individuals as whole persons rather than as compartmentalized intellectual or behavioral entities that they are not. The story method, particularized in life-situation illustrations, approaches individuals holistically and thus deals with people in a manner consistent with human learning, human speaking, and the scriptural tradition.

Notes

1. Alfred Schutz, *The Phenomenology of the Social World*, trans. George Walsh and Frederick Lehnert, Northwestern University Studies in Phenomenology and Existential Philosophy, ed. John Wild (Evanston, Ill.: Northwestern University Press, 1967), pp. 187, 195.
2. For an excellent concise summary of the development and claims of narrative theory in biblical studies see Alister E. McGrath, "The

Biography of God," *Christianity Today* 35 (July 22, 1991), pp. 22–24.

3. Aristotle, *The "Art" of Rhetoric*, Loeb Classical Library, trans. John Henry Freese, ed. T. E. Page et al. (Cambridge: Harvard University Press, 1926), p. 9.
4. *The Rhetoric of Aristotle*, trans. Lane Cooper (Englewood Cliffs, N.J.: Prentice-Hall, 1932), pp. 147, 149.
5. Ibid., p. 147.
6. *The Rhetoric of Aristotle*, pp. 5, 13, 147–49; James L. Golden, Goodwin F. Berquist, and William E. Coleman, *The Rhetoric of Western Thought*, 3d ed. (Dubuque, Ia.: Kendall/Hunt, 1983), p. 56.
7. *The Rhetoric of Aristotle*, p. 206.
8. Ibid., p. 209.
9. I. A. Richards, "Functions of and Factors in Language," in *The Rhetoric of Western Thought*, p. 206.
10. Ibid., p. 207.
11. Ibid., p. 193.
12. Ibid., p. 208.
13. Richards specifically applies this premise to the communication of religious principles (cf. *The Rhetoric of Western Thought*, p. 40).
14. Ibid., p. 92.
15. Kenneth Burke, *The Philosophy of Literary Form: Studies in Symbolic Action*, rev. ed. (New York: Vintage, 1957), p. 77.
16. Kenneth Burke, *A Grammar of Motives*, California ed. (Berkeley: University of California Press, 1969), p. 22.
17. Ibid., p. 23.
18. Kenneth Burke, *A Rhetoric of Motives*, California ed. (Berkeley: University of California Press, 1969), p. 112; *The Philosophy of Literary Form*, p. 111.
19. Burke, *A Grammar of Motives*, p. xv.
20. Fisher, "Narration as Human Communication Paradigm: The Case of Public Moral Argument," *Communication Monographs* 51 (1984), p. 3; Sonja K. Foss, Karen A. Foss, and Robert Trapp, "Ernesto Grassi," *Contemporary Perspectives on Rhetoric* (Prospect Heights, Ill.: Waveland, 1985), pp. 140–41.
21. Fisher, "Narration as Communication Paradigm," p. 6.
22. Burke, *A Grammar of Motives*, pp. xiv, 21; note also how Baumann specifically uses this Burkean analysis to demonstrate how illustrations may function in sermons (*An Introduction to Contemporary Preaching* [Grand Rapids: Baker, 1972], p. 250).
23. Fisher, "Narration as Communication Paradigm," p. 6.

24. Walter R. Fisher, "The Narrative Paradigm: An Elaboration," *Communication Monographs* 52 (1985), p. 350; "Narration as Communication Paradigm," pp. 3, 6, 8.

25. Rolf von Eckartsberg, "The Eco-Psychology of Personal Culture Building: An Existential Hermeneutic Approach," *Duquesne Studies in Phenomenological Psychology*, ed. Amadeo Giorgi, Richard Knowles, and David L. Smith (Atlantic Highlands, N.J.: Humanitas Press/Duquesne University Press, 1979), 3:243.

26. Ibid., 3:233.

27. Ibid.

28. Ibid.

29. Ibid., 3:238.

30. Michael J. Hyde, "Philosophical Hemeneutics and the Communication Experience: The Paradigm of Oral History," *Man and World* 13 (1980), p. 84.

31. Richard Lischer, "The Limits of Story," *Interpretation* 38 (January 1984), pp. 26–38.

32. Mention should also be made here of the wide use of narrative theory in biblical studies. Early works noting the character and importance of narrative in biblical communication include Eric Auerbach's *Mimesis: The Representation of Reality in Western Literature*, trans. Willard R. Trask (Princeton: Princeton University Press, 1942); H. Richard Niebuhr, *The Meaning of Revelation* (New York: Macmillan, 1941). Leland Ryken explores the genre characteristics of story that must be considered in biblical interpretation in *How to Read the Bible as Literature* (Grand Rapids: Zondervan, 1984). Robert Culley (*Studies in the Structure of Hebrew Narrative* [Philadelphia: Fortress, 1976]) and Peter Miscall (*The Workings of Old Testament Narrative* [Philadelphia: Fortress, 1983] both seek to uncover the unique ways in which narrative accounts preserve and transmit religious values. In a series of articles appearing in *Images of Man and God: Old Testament Short Stories in Literary Focus* (ed. Burke Long [Sheffield: Almond, 1981]), six writers attempt to describe the unique ways in which biblical stories elicit the power of emotional response in a way that cannot be duplicated by the intellectual formulation of doctrine. The nature of story becomes a hermeneutical tool in George Coats' *Genesis, with an Introduction to Narrative Literature* (Grand Rapids: Eerdmans, 1983) and in Michael Goldberg's *Jews and Christians, Getting Our Stories Straight: The Exodus and The Passion-Resurrection* (Nashville: Abingdon, 1985). Goldberg's work follows his previous groundbreaking effort in *Theology and Narrative* (Nashville: Parthenon, 1982), in which he sought to demonstrate that narrative is itself a type of systemization of theology not previously considered in the

systematics disciplines. Stanley Hauerwas steps further toward the practical in *Truthfulness and Tragedy: Further Investigations in Christian Ethics* (Notre Dame: University of Notre Dame Press, 1977) and in *A Community of Character: Toward a Constructive Christian Social Ethic* (Notre Dame: University of Notre Dame Press, 1981). In the earlier work Hauerwas establishes narrative as an alternative pattern for rationality in Christian ethics, and in the later work he applies that pattern to subjects as diverse as democratic politics, the church community, the family, sexual relationships, and abortion. In *Religion as Story* (ed. James Wiggins [New York: Harper & Row, 1975]), six authors deal with religious story in order to indicate the ways in which their thinking is informed and transformed by encounters with narrative.

33. Reuel Howe, *The Miracle of Dialogue* (New York: Seabury Press, 1963), p. 145.

34. Henry J. Eggold, *Preaching Is Dialogue: A Concise Introduction to Homiletics* (Grand Rapids: Baker, 1980), p. 14.

35. von Eckartsberg, "Eco-Psychology," p. 228.

36. Edmund A. Steimle, Morris J. Niedenthal, and Charles Rice, eds., *Preaching the Story* (Philadelphia: Fortress, 1980), p. 13.

Bibliography

Abbey, Merril R. *Preaching to the Contemporary Mind*. Nashville: Abingdon, 1963.

Adams, Jay E. *Preaching with Purpose: A Comprehensive Textbook on Biblical Preaching*. Grand Rapids: Baker, 1982.

_____. *Sense Appeal in the Sermons of Charles Haddon Spurgeon*. Studies in Preaching. Vol. 1. Nutley, N.J.: Presbyterian and Reformed, 1976.

Allen, Ronald J., and Thomas J. Herin. "Moving from The Story to Our Story." In *Preaching the Story*, ed. Edmund A. Steimle et al. (Philadelphia: Fortress, 1980), pp. 151–61.

Alsdurf, Phyllis. "Preaching at the Guthrie Theatre." *Christianity Today* 31 (July 10, 1987), pp. 58–60.

Alter, Robert. *The Art of Biblical Narrative*. New York: Basic Books, 1981.

Aristotle. *The "Art" of Rhetoric*. Trans. John Henry Freese. Ed. T. E. Page et al. Loeb Classical Library. Cambridge: Harvard University Press, 1959.

Auerbach, Erich. *Mimesis: The Representation of Reality in Western Literature*. Trans. Willard R. Trask. Princeton: Princeton University Press, 1953.

Baird, John E. *Preparing for Platform and Pulpit*. Nashville: Abingdon, 1968.

Barnhouse, Donald Grey. *Let Me Illustrate*. Westwood, N.J.: Revell, 1967.

Barr, James. *The Bible in the Modern World*. London: SCM, 1973.

Barrett, Ethel. *Storytelling: It's Easy.* Grand Rapids: Zondervan, 1960.

Bass, George M. *The Song and the Story.* Lima, Oh.: C.S.S., 1984.

——————. "The Story Sermon: Key to Effective Preaching." *Preaching* 2, 4 (1987), pp. 33–36.

Batcher, Elaine. *Emotion in the Classroom.* Praeger Studies in Ethnographic Perspectives on American Education. Gen. ed. Ray C. Rist. New York: Praeger, 1981.

Baumann, J. Daniel. *An Introduction to Contemporary Preaching.* Grand Rapids: Baker, 1972.

Bausch, William J. *Storytelling, Imagination and Faith.* Mystic, Conn.: Twenty-third, 1984.

Bergson, Henri. *An Introduction to Metaphysics.* Trans. T. E. Hulme. Indianapolis: Bobbs-Merrill, 1949.

Berlin, Adele. *Poetics and Biblical Interpretation.* The Bible and Literature Series. Sheffield: Almond, 1983.

Bloom, Benjamin S., ed. *Taxonomy of Educational Objectives: The Classification of Educational Goals.* Handbook I: Cognitive Domain. New York: David McKay, 1956.

Broadus, John A. *On the Preparation and Delivery of Sermons.* New York: Harper and Row, 1944.

Bryan, Dawson C. *The Art of Illustrating Sermons.* Nashville: Cokesbury, 1938.

Bryson, Harold T., and James C. Taylor. *Building Sermons to Meet People's Needs.* Nashville: Broadman, 1980.

Burke, Kenneth. *A Grammar of Motives.* California ed. Berkeley: University of California Press, 1969.

——————. *Language as Symbolic Action: Essays on Life, Literature and Method.* Berkeley: University of California Press, 1966.

——————. *The Philosophy of Literary Form: Studies in Symbolic Action.* Revised ed. New York: Vintage Books, 1957.

——————. *A Rhetoric of Motives.* California ed. Berkeley: University of California Press, 1969.

——————. *The Rhetoric of Religion: Studies in Logology.* Boston: Beacon, 1961.

Buttrick, David. *Homiletic.* Philadelphia: Fortress, 1987.

Coats, George. *Genesis, with an Introduction to Narrative Literature.* Grand Rapids: Eerdmans, 1983.

Collins, Clinton. "The Multiple Realities of Schooling." In *Existentialism and Phenomenology in Education: Collected Essays,* ed. David E. Denton (New York: Columbia University, Teacher's College Press, 1975), pp. 139–55.

Cooper, Lane, trans. *The Rhetoric of Aristotle.* Englewood Cliffs, N.J.: Prentice-Hall, 1932.

Cope, Edward Meredith. *The Rhetoric of Aristotle with a Commentary.* Ed. John Edwin Sandys. 3 vols. Cambridge, Eng.: Cambridge University Press, 1877.

Cox, James. *Preaching.* New York: Harper and Row, 1985.

Craddock, Fred B. *as one without authority.* Enid, Okla.: Phillips University Press, 1974.

————. *Overhearing the Gospel.* Nashville: Abingdon, 1979.

————. *Preaching.* Nashville: Abingdon, 1985.

Crenshaw, James. "The Contest of Darius' Guards." In *Images of God and Man: Old Testament Short Stories in Literary Focus,* ed. Burke O. Long; Bible and Literature Series (Sheffield: Almond, 1981), pp. 74–88.

Crites, Stephen. "Angels We Have Heard." In *Religion as Story,* ed. James B. Wiggins (New York: Harper and Row, 1975), pp. 23–63.

Culley, Robert C. *Studies in the Structure of Hebrew Narrative.* Philadelphia: Fortress, 1976.

Cyclopedia of Religious Anecdotes. Comp. James Gilchrist Lawson. Chicago: Revell, 1923.

Daane, James. *Preaching with Confidence.* Grand Rapids: Eerdmans, 1980.

Dabney, Robert L. *Sacred Rhetoric.* 1870; rpt. Carlisle, Pa.: Banner of Truth, 1979.

Danto, A. C. "Narration and Knowledge." *Philosophy and Literature* 6 (1982), pp. 17–32.

Davis, Dennis. "Notes for a Proseminar on Narrative Theory." Speech Communication Departmental Proseminar, Southern Illinois University at Carbondale, April 25, 1986.

Davis, Henry Grady. *Design for Preaching.* Philadelphia: Fortress, 1958.

Derrida, Jacques. "The Law of Genre." *Critical Inquiry* 7 (1980), pp. 55–81.

Eason, David L. "The New Journalism and the Image World: Two Modes of Organizing Experience." *Critical Studies in Mass Communication* 1 (1984), pp. 51–65.

Ebeling, Gerhard. "Word of God and Hermeneutic." In *The New Hermeneutic,* ed. James M. Robinson and John B. Cobb, Jr. (New York: Harper and Row, 1964), pp. 78–110.

Eggold, Henry J. *Preaching Is Dialogue: A Concise Introduction to Homiletics.* Grand Rapids: Baker, 1980.

Eizenga, Michael A. "One-Sided Versus Two-Sided Messages: An Examination of Communication Theory with Application to the Preaching Context." Ph.D. diss., Dallas Theological Seminary, 1983.

Ellingsen, Mark. *The Integrity of Biblical Narrative: Story in Theology and Proclamation.* Minneapolis: Fortress, 1990.

Embler, Weller. "Metaphor and Social Belief." *Et cetera* (Winter 1951). Reprinted in *Bridging Worlds Through General Semantics: Selections from Et cetera*, ed. Mary Morain (San Francisco: International Society for General Semantics, 1984), pp. 234–48.

Eslinger, Richard L. *A New Hearing: Living Options in Homiletic Method.* Nashville: Abingdon, 1987.

Fant, Clyde. *Preaching for Today.* New York: Harper and Row, 1977.

Fisher, Walter R. "Narration as a Human Communication Paradigm: The Case of Public Moral Argument." *Communication Monographs* 51 (1984), pp. 1–22.

––––––––. "The Narrative Paradigm: An Elaboration." *Communication Monographs* 52 (1985), pp. 347–67.

Flynn, Leslie B. *Come Alive with Illustrations: How to Find, Use and File Good Stories for Sermons and Speeches.* Grand Rapids: Baker, 1987.

Ford, D. W. Cleverly. *The Ministry of the Word.* Grand Rapids: Eerdmans, 1979.

Foss, Sonja K., Karen A. Foss, and Robert Trapp. "Ernesto Grassi." In *Contemporary Perspectives on Rhetoric* (Prospect Heights, Ill.: Waveland, 1985), pp. 125–51.

Foucault, Michel. *The Archaeology of Knowledge and the Discourse on Language.* Trans. A. M. Sheridan Smith. New York: Random House–Pantheon Books, 1972.

Frank, Armin Paul. *Kenneth Burke.* New York: Twayne, 1969.

Frentz, T. S., and T. B. Farrell. "Language-Action: A Paradigm for Communication." *The Quarterly Journal of Speech* 62 (1976), pp. 333–49.

Fuchs, Ernst. "The New Testament and the Hermeneutical Problem." In *The New Hermeneutic*, ed. James M. Robinson and John B. Cobb, Jr. (New York: Harper and Row, 1964), pp. 111–45.

Gagne, Robert M. *The Conditions of Learning.* 3d ed. New York: Holt, Rinehart and Winston, 1977.

Garrison, Webb B. *Creative Imagination in Preaching.* Nashville: Abingdon, 1960.

Gendlin, Eugene T. *Experience and the Creation of Meaning: A Philosophical and Psychological Approach to the Subjective.* New York: Free Press Glencoe, 1962.

Giorgi, Amedeo. "The Body: Focal Point of 20th Century Cultural Contradictions." *South Africa Journal of Psychology* 13 (1983), pp. 129–69.

––––––––. "Concerning the Possibility of Phenomenological Psychological Research." *Journal of Phenomenological Psychology* 14 (1984), pp. 129–69.

————. "Sketch of a Psychological Phenomenological Method." In *Phenomenology and Psychological Research*, ed. Amedeo Giorgi (Pittsburgh: Duquesne University Press, 1985), pp. 8–22.

Goldberg, Michael. *Jews and Christians, Getting Our Stories Straight: The Exodus and the Passion-Resurrection*. Nashville: Abingdon, 1985.

————. *Theology and Narrative*. Nashville: Parthenon, 1982.

Golden, James L., Goodwin F. Berquist, and William E. Coleman. *The Rhetoric of Western Thought*. 3d ed. Dubuque, Ia.: Kendall/Hunt, 1983.

Gordon, William J. *The Metaphorical Way of Learning and Knowing: Applying Synectics to Sensitivity and Learning Situations*. 2d ed. Cambridge, Mass.: Porpoise Books, 1973.

————. *Synectics: The Development of Creative Capacity*. New York: Collier, 1968.

Grassi, Ernesto. *Rhetoric as Philosophy: The Humanist Tradition*. University Park: Pennsylvania State University Press, 1980.

Greidanus, Sidney. *Sola Scriptura: Problems and Principles in Preaching Historical Texts*. Toronto: Wedge Publishing Foundation, 1970.

Gunn, David. "A Man Given Over to Trouble: The Story of King Saul." In *Images of God and Man: Old Testament Short Stories in Literary Focus*, ed. Burke O. Long; Bible and Literature Series (Sheffield: Almond, 1981), pp. 89–112.

Hall, Thor. *The Future Shape of Preaching*. Philadelphia: Fortress, 1971.

Hauerwas, Stanley. *A Community of Character: Toward a Constructive Christian Ethic*. Notre Dame: University of Notre Dame Press, 1981.

Hauerwas, Stanley, with Richard Bondi and David B. Burrell. *Truthfulness and Tragedy: Further Investigations in Christian Ethics*. Notre Dame: University of Notre Dame Press, 1977.

Hergenhahn, B. R. *An Introduction to Theories of Learning*. Englewood Cliffs, N.J.: Prentice-Hall, 1976.

Hilgard, Ernest R., and Gordon H. Bower. *Theories of Learning*. 5th ed. Englewood Cliffs, N.J.: Prentice-Hall, 1981.

Hill, Winfred F. *Learning: A Survey of Psychological Interpretations*. Rev. ed. Scranton, Pa.: Chandler, 1971.

Hostetler, Michael J. *Introducing the Sermon: The Art of Compelling Beginnings*. Grand Rapids: Zondervan, 1986.

Howe, Reuel. *The Miracle of Dialogue*. New York: Seabury, 1963.

Hyde, Michael J. "Philosophical Hermeneutics and the Communicative Experience: The Paradigm of Oral History." *Man and World* 13 (1980), pp. 81–98.

Inch, Morris A., gen. ed. *The Literature and Meaning of Scripture*. Grand Rapids: Baker, 1981.

Jackson, Edgar N. *A Psychology for Preaching.* Great Neck, N.Y.: Channel, 1961.

Jaynes, Julian. *The Origin of Consciousness in the Breakdown of the Bicameral Mind.* Boston: Houghton Mifflin., 1976.

Johnson, Byron Val. "A Media Selection Model for Use with a Homiletical Taxonomy." Ph.D. diss., Carbondale: Southern Illinois University, 1982.

Johnson, Wendell. *People in Quandaries: The Semantics of Personal Adjustment.* New York: Harper and Brothers., 1946.

Jones, Ilion T. *Principles and Practice of Preaching.* Nashville: Abingdon, 1956.

Kearney, Richard, ed. *Dialogues with Contemporary Continental Thinkers: The Phenomenological Heritage.* Manchester, Eng.: Manchester University Press, 1984.

Kemp, Charles F. *Life-Situation Preaching.* St. Louis: Bethany, 1956.

_____. *Pastoral Preaching.* St. Louis: Bethany, 1963.

Kemper, Deane. *Effective Preaching.* Philadelphia: Westminster, 1985.

Kermode, F. "Secrets and Narrative Sequence." *Critical Inquiry* 7 (1980), pp. 83–101.

Killinger, John. *Fundamentals of Preaching.* Philadelphia: Fortress, 1985.

Kirkwood, W. G. "Storytelling and Self-confrontation: Parables as Communication Strategies." *The Quarterly Journal of Speech* 69 (1983), pp. 58–74.

Klausmeier, Herbert J., Elizabeth Schwenn Ghatala, and Dorothy A. Frayer. *Conceptual Learning and Development: A Cognitive View.* New York: Academic Press, 1974.

Klooster, Fred. *Quests for the Historical Jesus.* Grand Rapids: Craig, 1966.

Korzybski, Alfred. *Science and Sanity.* Lakeville, Conn.: International Non-Aristotelian Library, 1958.

Kowalzik, John F. G. "A Cognitive-Linguistic Prototype for Speech Analysis." Ph.D. diss., Carbondale: Southern Illinois University, 1970.

Kraft, Charles H. *Communicating the Gospel God's Way.* Pasadena: William Carey Library, 1979.

Kroll, Woodrow Michael. *Prescription for Preaching.* Grand Rapids: Baker, 1980.

Lambertson, John Paul. "The Theory of Sermon Illustration as Revealed in Textbooks and Other Pertinent Writings on Preaching, 1880–1955." Ph.D. diss., Pittsburgh: University of Pittsburgh, 1959.

Lane, Belden C. "Rabbinical Stories: A Primer on Theological 'MB Method." *The Christian Century* 98 (1981), pp. 1306–10.

————. "Reflections on Narrative Preaching: Why We Never Fall Asleep in Stories." Lecture recorded in St. Louis, Mo., by Concordia Seminary Media Services, 1984. (Cass. 83–28).

Lanigan, Richard L. "Communication Models in Philosophy: Review and Commentary." In *International Communication Association Yearbook 3*, ed. Dan Nimmo (New Brunswick: Transaction Books, 1979), pp. 29–49.

————. "Enthymeme: The Rhetorical Species of Aristotle's Syllogism." *The Southern Speech Communication Journal* 39 (1974), pp. 207–22.

————. "Maurice Merleau-Ponty." *Encyclopedic Dictionary of Semiotics*, ed. Thomas Sebeok (Berlin: de Gruyter, 1987), vol. 1.

————. "Phenomenology." *Encyclopedic Dictionary of Semiotics*, ed. Thomas Sebeok (Berlin: de Gruyter, 1987), vol. 2, pp. 564–67.

————. "The Phenomenology of Human Communication." *Philosophy Today* 23 (1979), pp. 3–15.

Lehman, Louis Paul. *Put a Door on It*. Grand Rapids: Kregel, 1975.

Lenski, R. C. H. *The Sermon: Its Homiletical Construction*. Grand Rapids: Baker, 1968 (original, 1927).

Leuking, F. Dean. *Preaching: The Art of Connecting God and People*. Waco, Tex.: Word, 1985.

Levin, David Michael, *The Body's Recollection of Being: Phenomenological Psychology and the Deconstruction of Nihilism*. London: Routledge and Kegan Paul, 1985.

Lewis, Ralph. *Speech for Persuasive Preaching*. Wilmore, Ky.: Lewis, 1968.

————. "The Triple Brain Test of a Sermon." *Preaching* 1, 2 (1985), pp. 9–12.

Lewis, Ralph, with Gregg Lewis. *Inductive Preaching*. Westchester, Ill.: Crossway, 1983.

Lischer, Richard. "The Limits of Story." *Interpretation* 38 (January 1984), pp. 26–38.

Liske, Thomas V. *Effective Preaching*. New York: MacMillan, 1960.

Litfin, Duane. "The Five Most-Used Homiletics Texts." *Christianity Today* 17 (1973), p. 1138.

Logan, Samuel T., Jr. "The Phenomenology of Preaching." In *The Preacher and Preaching: Reviving the Art in the Twentieth Century*, ed. Samuel T. Logan, Jr. (Phillipsburg, N.J.: Presbyterian and Reformed, 1986), pp. 129–60.

————., ed. *The Preacher and Preaching: Reviving the Art in the Twentieth Century*. Phillipsburg, N.J.: Presbyterian and Reformed, 1986.

Long, Burke O. *Images of Man and God: Old Testament Short Stories in Literary Focus*. Sheffield: Almond, 1981.

Lowery, Eugene L. *Doing Time in the Pulpit: The Relationship Between Narrative and Preaching.* Nashville: Abingdon, 1985.
_____. *The Homiletical Plot: The Sermon as Narrative Art Form.* Atlanta: John Knox, 1980.
_____. *How to Preach a Parable: Designs for Narrative Sermons.* Nashville: Abingdon, 1989.
Lyne, J. "Discourse, Knowledge and Social Process: Some Changing Equations." *The Quarterly Journal of Speech* 68 (1982), pp. 201–14.
MacCormac, E. R. *Metaphor and Myth in Science and Religion.* Durham, N.C.: Duke University Press, 1976.
MacPherson, Ian. *The Art of Illustrating Sermons.* Nashville: Abingdon, 1964.
Mannebach, Wayne C., and Joseph M. Mazza. *Speaking from the Pulpit.* Valley Forge, Pa.: Judson, 1969.
Marquart, Edward F. *Quest for Better Preaching.* Minneapolis: Augsburg, 1985.
Matson, Floyd, and Ashley Montagu. "The Unfinished Revolution." In *The Human Dialogue: Perspectives on Communication*, ed. Floyd W. Matson and Ashley Montagu (New York: Free Press, 1967), pp. 1–11.
McEachern, Alton H. "A New Look at Narrative Preaching." *Preaching* 1, 1 (1985), pp. 11–13.
McGee, M. C., and M. A. Martin. "Public Knowledge and Ideological Argumentation." *Communication Monographs* 50 (1983), pp. 47–65.
McGrath, Alister E. "The Biography of God." *Christianity Today* 35 (July 22, 1991), pp. 22–24.
McGuire, Errol. "The Joseph Story: A Tale of Son and Father." In *Images of God and Man: Old Testament Short Stories in Literary Focus*, ed. Burke O. Long; Bible and Literature Series (Sheffield: Almond, 1981), pp. 9–25.
Merleau-Ponty, Maurice. *Phenomenology of Perception.* Trans. Colin Smith with revisions by Forrest Williams. London, 1962; rpt. Atlantic Highlands, N.J.: Humanities Press, 1981.
_____. *In Praise of Philosophy.* Trans. John Wild and James Edie. Northwestern University Studies in Phenomenology and Existential Philosophy. Evanston: Northwestern University Press, 1963.
_____. *The Prose of the World.* Trans. John O'Neill. Ed. Claude Lefort. Evanston: Northwestern University Press, 1973.
_____. *Themes from the Lectures at the Collège de France 1952–1960.* Trans. John O'Neill. Evanston, Ill.: Northwestern University Press, 1970.
Mink, L. O. "Narrative Form as Cognitive Instrument." In *The Writing of History*, ed. R. H. Canary (Madison: University of Wisconsin Press, 1978), pp. 129–49.

Miscall, Peter D. *The Workings of Old Testament Narrative*. Philadelphia: Fortress, 1983.

Mitchell, Henry H. *The Recovery of Preaching*. New York: Harper and Row, 1977.

Mohler, R. Albert, Jr. "Past Year Produced Outstanding Books for Preaching." *Preaching* 2, 4 (1987), pp. 4–8.

Mudge, Lewis S., "Paul Ricoeur on Biblical Interpretation." In *Essays on Biblical Interpretation*, ed. Lewis S. Mudge (Philadelphia: Fortress, 1980), pp. 1–40.

Murphy, James J. *Medieval Rhetoric: A Select Bibliography*. Toronto: University of Toronto Press, 1971.

_____. *Rhetoric in the Middle Ages: A History of Rhetorical Theory from Saint Augustine to the Renaissance*. Berkeley: University of California Press, 1974.

Nichols, Marie Hochmuth. "Kenneth Burke and the 'New Rhetoric.'" In *The Rhetoric of Western Thought*, ed. James Golden, Goodwin Berquist, and William Coleman, 2d ed. (Dubuque, Ia.: Kendall-Hunt, 1976), pp. 236–50.

Niebuhr, H. Richard. *The Meaning of Revelation*. New York: Macmillan, 1941.

Nohrnberg, James. "Moses." In *Images of God and Man: Old Testament Short Stories in Literary Focus*, ed. Burke O. Long, Bible and Literature Series (Sheffield: Almond, 1981), pp. 74–88.

Novak, Michael. "Story and Experience." In *Religion as Story*, ed. James B. Wiggins (New York: Harper and Row, 1975), pp. 175–200.

Oates, Wayne E. "Preaching to Emotional Needs." *Preaching* 1, 5 (1985), pp. 5–7.

Ogden, C. K., and I. A. Richards. *The Meaning of Meaning: A Study of the Influence of Language Upon Thought and of the Science of Symbolism*. 4th ed. New York: Harcourt, Brace and Co., 1936.

Ong, Walter J. *Orality and Literacy: The Technologizing of the Word*. London: Methuen, 1982.

Palmer, Richard. *Hermeneutics*. Evanston: Northwestern University Press, 1969.

Perelman, Chaim, and L. Olbrechts-Tyteca. *The New Rhetoric*. Trans. John Wilkinson and Purcell Weaver. Notre Dame: University of Notre Dame Press, 1969.

Perry, Lloyd M. *A Manual for Biblical Preaching*. Grand Rapids: Baker, 1965.

Perry, Lloyd M., and Charles M. Sell. *Speaking to Life's Problems*. Chicago: Moody, 1983.

Perry, Lloyd M., and John R. Strubhar. *Evangelistic Preaching*. Chicago: Moody Press, 1979.

Pitt-Watson, Ian. *A Primer for Preachers*. Grand Rapids: Baker, 1986.

Powell, Mark Alan. *What Is Narrative Criticism?* Minneapolis: Fortress, 1990.

Quale, William A. *The Pastor-Preacher*, ed. Warren Wiersbe. Grand Rapids: Baker, 1979.

Ramm, Bernard. *Protestant Biblical Interpretation: A Textbook of Hermeneutics*. Grand Rapids: Baker, 1970.

Regan, Catharine A. "Liturgy and Preaching as Oral Context for Medieval English Literature." In *Performance of Literature in Historical Perspectives*, ed. David W. Thompson (New York: University Press, 1983), pp. 147–75.

Richards, I. A. "Functions of and Factors in Language." In *The Rhetoric of Western Thought*, ed. James Golden et al., 3d ed. (Dubuque, Ia.: Kendall/Hunt, 1983), pp. 200–210.

————. *The Philosophy of Rhetoric*. New York: Oxford University Press, 1936.

Ricoeur, Paul. "The Hermeneutics of Testimony." In *Essays on Biblical Interpretation*, ed. Lewis S. Mudge (Philadelphia: Fortress, 1980), pp. 119–54.

————. *Interpretation Theory: Discourse and the Surplus of Meaning*. Fort Worth: Texas Christian University Press, 1976.

————. "The Narrative Function." In *Paul Ricoeur, Hermeneutics and the Human Sciences: Essays on Language, Action and Interpretation*, ed. J. B. Thompson (Cambridge: Cambridge University Press, 1983), pp. 274–96.

————. "Narrative Time." *Critical Inquiry* 7 (1980), pp. 169–90.

Ringness, Thomas. *The Affective Domain in Education*. Boston: Little, Brown and Co., 1975.

Robertson, A. T. *Word Pictures in the New Testament*. Nashville: Broadman, 1932.

Robertson, James D. "Sermon Illustration and the Use of Resources." In *Baker's Dictionary of Practical Theology*, ed. Ralph G. Turnbull (Grand Rapids: Baker, 1967). Reprinted in *Homiletics* (Grand Rapids: Baker, 1972), pp. 44–56.

Robinson, Haddon. *Biblical Preaching: The Development and Delivery of Expository Messages*. Grand Rapids: Baker, 1980.

Robinson, James M. "Hermeneutic Since Barth." In *The New Hermeneutic*, vol. 2 of *New Frontiers in Theology: Discussions Among Continental and American Theologians*, ed. James M. Robinson and John B. Cobb, Jr. (New York: Harper and Row, 1964), pp. 1–77.

Robinson, Wayne Bradley, ed. *Journeys toward Narrative Preaching*. New York: Pilgrim, 1990.

Rosenberg, Bruce A. *The Art of the American Folk Preacher*. New York: Oxford University Press, 1970.

Rueckert, William. *Kenneth Burke and the Drama of Human Relations.* Minneapolis: University of Minnesota Press, 1963.

Runia, Klaas. "Experience in the Reformed Tradition." *Theological Forum of the Reformed Ecumenical Synod* 15, nos. 2 & 3 (April, 1987), pp. 7–13.

Ruopp, Harold W. "Life Situation Preaching." *The Christian Century Pulpit* 12 (1941), pp. 116–17.

————. "Life Situation Preaching (Part II)." *The Christian Century Pulpit* 12 (1941), pp. 140–41.

————. "Preaching to Life Situations." *The Christian Century Pulpit* 6 (1935), pp. 20–21.

Ryken, Leland. *How to Read the Bible as Literature.* Grand Rapids: Zondervan, 1984.

Salmon, Bruce C. *Storytelling in Preaching: A Guide to the Theory and Practice.* Nashville: Broadman, 1988.

Sanderson, John W. *Mirrors of His Glory: Images of God from Scripture.* Phillipsburg, N.J.: Presbyterian and Reformed, 1990.

Sangster, W. E. *The Craft of Sermon Construction.* Grand Rapids: Baker, 1972.

————. *The Craft of Sermon Illustration.* London: Epworth, 1948.

————. *The Craft of the Sermon.* London: Epworth, 1954.

Schlafer, David J. "Narrative Preaching Under Fire." Papers of the Annual Meeting of the Academy of Homiletics (1990), pp. 111–21.

Schraq, Calvin O. *Experience and Being.* Evanston, Ill.: Northwestern University Press, 1969.

Schutz, Alfred. *The Phenomenology of the Social World.* Trans. George Walsh and Frederick Lehnert. Northwestern University Studies in Phenomenology and Existential Philosophy. Evanston, Ill.: Northwestern University Press, 1967.

Shoemaker, Stephen H. *Retelling the Biblical Story: The Theology and Practice of Narrative Preaching.* Nashville: Broadman, 1985.

Simons, H. C. "In Praise of Muddleheaded Anecdotalism." *Western Journal of Speech Communication* 42 (1978), pp. 21–28.

Smick, Elmer B. "Preaching from the Psalms." *Presbyterian Journal* 45 (February 4, 1987), pp. 9–11.

Smith, Frank. *Comprehension and Learning.* New York: Holt, Rinehart and Winston, 1975.

Spiegelberg, Herbert. *Phenomenology in Psychology and Psychiatry: A Historical Introduction.* Northwestern University Studies in Phenomenology and Existential Philosophy. Evanston: Northwestern University Press, 1972.

Spurgeon, C. H. *The Art of Illustration.* Third Series of *Lectures to My Students.* London: Marshall Brothers, 1922.

————. *Flowers from a Puritan's Garden*. Westwood, 1883; rpt. Harrisonburg, Va.: Sprinkle, 1976.

Steimle, Edmund A., Morris J. Niedenthal, and Charles Rice, eds. *Preaching the Story*. Philadelphia: Fortress, 1980.

Steinaker, Norman, and Robert M. Bell. "A Proposed Taxonomy of Educational Objectives: The Experiential Domain." *Educational Technology* 15 (1975), pp. 14–16.

Sternberg, Meir. *The Poetics of Biblical Narrative: Ideological Literature and the Drama of Reading*. Indiana Literary Biblical Series. Bloomington, Ind.: Indiana University Press, 1985.

Stott, John R. W. *Between Two Worlds: The Art of Preaching in the Twentieth Century*. Grand Rapids: Eerdmans, 1982.

Strasser, Stephan. *Phenomenology of Feeling*. Trans. Robert E. Wood. Philosophy Series, vol. 34. Pittsburgh: Duquesne University Press, 1977.

Swindoll, Charles. *Come Before Winter and Share My Hope*. Portland: Multnomah Press, 1985.

Thiselton, Anthony C. *The Two Horizons: New Testament Philosophical Description with Special Reference to Heidegger, Bultmann, Godamer and Wittgenstein*. Grand Rapids: Eerdmans, 1980.

Thompson, William D., and Gordon C. Bennett. *Dialogue Preaching: The Shared Sermon*. Valley Forge, Pa.: Judson, 1969.

Troeger, Thomas H. *Imagining a Sermon*. Nashville: Abingdon, 1990.

Turnbull, Ralph G., ed. *Baker's Dictionary of Practical Theology*. Grand Rapids: Baker, 1967.

Turner, V. "Social Dramas and Stories About Them." *Critical Inquiry* 7 (1980), pp. 141–68.

20 Centuries of Great Preaching. Ed. Clyde E. Fant, Jr., and William M. Pinson, Jr. Vol. 12. Waco, Tex.: Word, 1971.

Ulbrich, Armand H. "The Use of Illustrations in Christian Preaching." Master's thesis, St. Louis: Concordia Theological Seminary, 1938.

Van Der Geest, Hans. *Presence in the Pulpit: The Impact of Personality in Preaching*. Trans. Douglas W. Stott. Atlanta: John Knox, 1981.

Van Til, Cornelius. *A Christian Theory of Knowledge*. Nutley, N.J.: Presbyterian and Reformed., 1969.

VanOosting, James. "Moses, Hezekiah and Yale's Gang of Four." *The Reformed Journal*, 33 (November 1983), pp. 7–8.

von Eckartsberg, Rolf. "An Approach to Experiential Social Psychology." In *Duquesne Studies in Phenomenological Psychology*, vol. 1, ed. Amadeo Giorgi, W. F. Fisher, and Rolf von Eckartsberg (Pittsburgh: Duquesne University Press, 1971), pp. 325–71.

————. "The Eco-Psychology of Personal Culture Building: An Existential Hermeneutic Approach." In *Duquesne Studies in Phenomenological Psychology*, vol. 3, ed. Amadeo Giorgi, Richard

Knowles, and David L. Smith (Atlantic Highlands, N.J.: Humanitas Press/Duquesne University Press, 1979), pp. 227–44.

————. "Encounter as the Basic Unit of Social Interaction." *Humanities* 1, 2 (1965), pp. 195–214.

————. "On Experiential Methodology." In *Duquesne Studies in Phenomenological Psychology*, vol. 1, ed. Amedeo Giorgi, W. F. Fisher, and Rolf von Eckartsberg (Pittsburgh: Duquesne University Press, 1971), pp. 66–79.

Wardlaw, James M., ed. *Preaching Biblically: Creating Sermons in the Shape of Scripture*. Philadelphia: Westminster, 1983.

Welsh, Clement. *Preaching in a New Key: Studies in the Psychology of Thinking and Listening*. Philadelphia: United Church Press, 1974.

White, Hayden. *The Tropics of Discourse: Essays in Cultural Criticism*. Baltimore: Johns Hopkins University Press, 1978.

————. "The Value of Narrativity in the Representation of Reality." *Critical Inquiry* 7 (1980), pp. 5–27.

White, R. E. O. *A Guide to Preachers*. Grand Rapids: Eerdmans, 1973.

Whitesell, Faris D. *Power in Expository Preaching*. Westwood, N.J.: Revell, 1963.

Wiggins, James B., ed. *Religion as Story*. New York: Harper and Row, 1975.

Williams, David A. "From Academic to Psycho-Social Uses of Literature." In *Performance of Literature in Historical Perspectives*, ed. David W. Thompson (New York: University Press, 1983), pp. 419–35.

Williams, James G. *Women Recounted: Narrative Thinking and the God of Israel*. Sheffield: Almond, 1981.

Williams, Linda Verlee. *Teaching for the Two-Sided Mind*. Englewood Cliffs, N.J.: Prentice-Hall, 1983.

Willimon, William H. "Preaching: Entertainment or Exposition?" *The Christian Century* 107 (February 28, 1990), pp. 204–6.

Wilson, John F., and Carroll C. Arnold. *Public Speaking as Liberal Art*. Boston: Allyn and Bacon, 1978.

Wilson, Joseph Ruggles. "In What Sense Are Preachers to Preach Themselves?" *Southern Presbyterian Review* 25 (1874), pp. 350–60.

Wolff, Norman. "The Use of Illustrations in Sermons." Master's thesis, St. Louis: Concordia Theological Seminary, 1945.

Wyer, Robert S., Jr. *Cognitive Organization and Change: An Information Processing Approach*. Potomac, Md.: Lawrence Erlbaum Associates, 1974.

General Index

Adams, Jay, 32–33, 37, 99, 110
Akibu, Rabbi, 80
Allegory problems, 24–25
Aristotle, 192
Auerbach, Eric, 203

Barnhouse, Donald Grey, 103, 131
Barrett, Ethel, 34
Bauman, J. Daniel, 31, 35, 162
Biblical narrative, 41
Broadus, John, 22
Bronze serpent, 76ff.
Bryan, Dawson C., 68, 85, 99, 106, 125, 128, 171
Bryan, William Jennings, 21
Burke, Kenneth, 194ff.

Calhoun, David, 44, 126
Calvin, John, 65 66
Chappell, Clovis, 21
Coats, George, 203
Counseling confidences, 169–70
Covenant symbols, 40ff.
Craddock, Fred B., 26, 31, 113
Crisis, 122ff.
Crites, Stephen, 85–86
Culley, Robert, 203
Cyrus, 106

Dale, Edgar, 54
Davis, Henry Grady, 22
Dowling, John, 85

Edwards, Jonathan, 21
Eggold, Henry, 198
Ellingsen, Mark, 35
Emotions, 36ff.

Eslinger, Richard, 35
Ethos, 142ff., 151

Farley, Frederick, 160–67
Fisher, Walter, 33, 196ff.
Fletcher, Lionel, 114
Flynn, Leslie, 185
Fosdick, Harry Emerson, 21

Gagne, Robert, 52
Garrison, Webb, 113, 118–19
Gay, John, 162
Gestalt theorists, 51
Goldberg, Michael, 71–72, 203
Graham, Billy, 114
Grassi, Ernesto, 72–73
Grouping statements, 131ff.
Gunn, David, 85
Guthrie, Edwin Ray, 51

Haggadah, 43
Halakah, 43
Hauerwas, Stanley, 71, 85–86, 203–4
Hezekiah, 77
Historical narrative, 41
Horton, R. F., 153
Howe, Reuel, 18, 198
Human interest accounts, 29, 53, 55, 60, 80
Humor, 163ff.

Illustration defined, 19–20
Illustration hierarchy, 18–19
Inductive preaching, 26ff.
Interpreting statements, 131ff.
Ironside, Harry, 121

Jackson, Edgar N., 97

Index of Illustrations

Scripture Index